innovativ
unterrichten

Vikas Swarup

Q & A – Slumdog Millionaire

Eine Unterrichtseinheit für die Oberstufe

mit CD-ROM

STARK

Vikas Swarup, Q&A – *Slumdog Millionaire*

eine Unterrichtseinheit für die Oberstufe
von Judith Christina Säckl

Liebe Lehrerinnen,
liebe Lehrer,

Indien – Land der Maharadschas und Paläste, schillernd-bizarre Welt Bollywoods und aufstrebende Wirtschaftsregion, in der aber auch Millionen Menschen in bitterster Armut leben. Trotz oder vielleicht gerade wegen dieser Kontraste packt viele Menschen das Fernweh beim Gedanken an den Subkontinent – bestimmt auch einige Ihrer Schüler. Mit der Behandlung des Romans *Q & A* von Vikas Swarup können Sie Ihre Klasse zumindest auf eine imaginäre Reise mitnehmen und gemeinsam in die fremde Kultur eintauchen. Durch **Einbezug der Verfilmung** *Slumdog Millionaire* erhalten die Schüler darüber hinaus einen visuellen Input, was ihnen eine affektive Annäherung an die Themenkomplexe und ein Einfühlen in die Charaktere erheblich erleichtert.

Gemeinsam mit dem Protagonisten Ram bzw. der Filmfigur Jamal entdecken die Schüler zahlreiche Facetten Indiens, auch abseits der großen Sehenswürdigkeiten, und erhalten so Einblick in das Leben und die Probleme der unterschiedlichen sozialen Schichten Indiens. So ermöglicht die Lektüre eine kritische Auseinandersetzung mit der fremden Kultur.

Die Struktur des Buches wird auf die thematische Gliederung der Unterrichtseinheit übertragen: Wie sich durch die Antworten auf die Quizfragen langsam das Bild von Rams Lebensgeschichte zusammensetzt, so erhalten die Schüler anhand der Beschäftigung mit neun unterschiedlichen Themenbereichen Einblick in die indische Kultur. **Handlungsorientierte Arbeitsaufträge** fordern zudem auf zu mehr Schüleraktivität und einer kreativen Auseinandersetzung mit der Lektüre. Zudem finden Sie **digitales Zusatzmaterial** auf der beiliegenden CD-ROM:

- **Videoclip** zur Veranschaulichung der Situation im größten indischen Slum Dharavi
- eine **MP3-Datei** zur musikalischen Untermalung einer Sequenz aus dem Film *Slumdog Millionaire*
- alle **Kopiervorlagen in PDF- und Word-Versionen** zur individuellen Anpassung

Ich wünschen Ihnen und Ihren Schülern interessante Englischstunden mit *Q & A* und *Slumdog Millionaire*!

Judith Christina Säckl

Einführung

Warum Q & A?

Kaum ein anderer zeitgenössischer Roman zum Thema Indien umfasst so viele Aspekte der indischen Gesellschaft wie *Q & A* von Vikas Swarup. Durch deren Einbettung in eine **spannende Handlungsführung** fühlt sich der Leser von der Vielfalt an Themen aber keineswegs erschlagen und überfordert. Ihm bietet sich vielmehr die Chance mit den Charakteren eine **Reise durch das „äußere" und „innere" Indien** zu unternehmen – durch die Landschaften und Städte, aber auch durch die Gefühle und Gedanken der Menschen. Diese Vielfalt und Anschaulichkeit des Romans ermöglicht einen sowohl kognitiven als auch affektiven Zugang zum indischen Subkontinent. So verwundert es nicht, dass die Verfilmung des Romans unter dem Titel *Slumdog Millionaire* acht Oscars erhielt und als Kassenschlager weltweit die Kinos eroberte.

Die vorliegende Sequenz ist für den Englischunterricht der Oberstufe geeignet und fördert die Schüler auf vielseitige Weise. Obwohl der Fokus auf der Lektüre des Romans liegt, wird der Bezug zur Filmversion *Slumdog Millionaire* zur Veranschaulichung mehrmals hergestellt: Der **Vergleich von Romanvorlage und Filmversion** sowie die Auseinandersetzung mit den Reaktionen auf *Slumdog Millionaire* rundet die Einheit ab.

Q & A bietet für die Schüler **vielfältige Identifikationsmöglichkeiten.** Charaktere verschiedenen Alters aus unterschiedlichen Schichten und Religionen treten auf und vermitteln somit ein sehr breit gefächertes Bild des Landes. Die Schüler werden gemeinsam mit dem Protagonisten Ram Zeugen des Luxuslebens der Bollywood-Schauspieler, tauchen ein in die Kreise der internationalen Diplomatie und lernen die Trostlosigkeit der Waisenhäuser und Slums kennen: Arm und Reich treffen aufeinander, Frauen erzählen von ihrer Situation, wodurch deren untergeordnete Stellung innerhalb der Gesellschaft aufgezeigt wird; Kinder kämpfen mit- und gegeneinander ums Überleben, Nachbarn nutzen sich aus oder helfen einander.

Inhalt und Aufbau des Romans

Der Roman *Q & A* erzählt von der Kindheit und Jugend des indischen Straßenjungen Ram Mohammad Thomas, der als Waise aufwächst und durch Zufall und Gelegenheitsjobs Einblick in viele Schichten und Lebensbedingungen der indischen Gesellschaft erhält. Viele seiner Erlebnisse teilt er mit Salim, seinem besten Freund, den er im Waisenhaus kennenlernt und mit dem er zeitweise zusammenwohnt.

Diese Lebensgeschichte wird episodenhaft erzählt und ist eingebettet in eine Rahmenhandlung. Ram hat an der Quizshow „Who Will Win a Billion?" teilgenommen und die Höchstsumme gewonnen. Da ihm niemand glaubt, dass er als einfacher, ungebildeter Straßenjunge und Gelegenheitsarbeiter die Antworten auf alle Fragen gewusst haben kann, wird er des Betrugs beschuldigt und festgenommen. Die Produzenten der Show verfügen zudem gar nicht über die Gewinnsumme und hatten absichtlich einen ungebildeten Straßenjungen als Kandidaten ausgewählt. Die Anwältin Smita Shah nimmt sich jedoch Rams an und setzt es sich zum Ziel, zu jeder Frage die Umstände herauszufinden, die ihm die richtige Beantwortung ermöglichten. So erzählt Ram ihr seine Lebensgeschichte. Er folgt dabei nicht der chronologischen Reihenfolge der Geschehnisse, sondern der Abfolge der Fragen in der Quizshow. So erzählt er beispielsweise von den Jahren, in denen er als kleines Kind bei einem englischen Priester lebte, von seiner Zeit im Waisenhaus oder von seinen vielen verschiedenen Gelegenheitsjobs

(z. B. als Kellner in Mumbai, als Fremdenführer am Taj Mahal in Agra, als Hausange-stellter bei der alternden Bollywood-Schauspielerin Neelima Kumari und im Haus eines australischen Diplomaten). In Agra lernt er Nita kennen und lieben, die von ihrer Familie zur Prostitution gezwungen wird. Ram will sie befreien und heiraten, doch ihr Bruder und Zuhälter fordert immer mehr Geld von ihm. Um diese Summe aufzubrin-gen, entschließt sich Ram, an der Quizshow teilzunehmen. Ein weiterer Grund für seine Teilnahme ist sein ursprünglicher Plan, den Showmaster Prem Kumar umzubrin-gen, der sowohl Neelima Kumari als auch Nita missbrauchte. Nita misshandelte er so schwer, dass sie auf der Intensivstation landete. Nach den Vorgaben der Show darf der Showmaster den Kandidaten nie alleine lassen und so wollte Ram ihn auf der Toilette umbringen. Ram lässt schließlich doch von diesem Vorhaben ab und zum Dank verrät ihm Prem Kumar die Antwort auf die letzte Frage, die einzige, die er vielleicht wirklich nicht hätte beantworten können.

Jedes der zwölf Kapitel des Romans endet mit einer Quizfrage, die Ram durch seine zuvor beschriebenen Erlebnisse beantworten kann. Durch diese Struktur haben die einzelnen Kapitel Kurzgeschichtencharakter und widmen sich jeweils einem thema-tischen Schwerpunkt.

Vergleich von Roman und Film Während die Handlung des Romans in Episoden erzählt wird, deren Rahmenhandlung die Quizshow bildet, verläuft die Geschichte von Jamal K. Malik (wie Ram in der Ver-filmung *Slumdog Millionaire* heißt) chronologisch. Zudem ergeben sich auch einige in-haltliche Veränderungen: im Film sind Jamal und Salim **Brüder statt Freunde**. Wäh-rend der Protagonist von *Q & A* alle drei Religionen in seinem Namen vereint, sind die Maliks im Film **Moslems. Jamal und Latika kennen sich bereits von Kindesbei-nen an**, während Ram die Prostituierte Nita erst mit 17 Jahren trifft. Salim und Jamal halten sich im Film nur in Mumbai und Agra (in der Nähe des Taj Mahal) auf, in *Q & A* kommt mit New Delhi noch ein dritter Handlungsort hinzu. Während die **Quizshow** im Film **live** übertragen wird, wird sie im Roman aufgezeichnet. Sowohl der **Name der Sendung** als auch die **Anzahl und Art der Fragen** wurden für *Slumdog Millionaire* ge-ändert. Im Film findet **Jamals Verhaftung** bereits **vor der letzten Frage** statt. Jamals Telefonjoker ist sein Bruder Salim, der aber sein Handy mittlerweile an Latika weiterge-geben hat. Der Authentizität willen werden **viele Dialoge** in *Slumdog Millionaire* **auf Hindi** geführt.

Die beiden Grafiken auf der folgenden Seite vermitteln eine **Übersicht über den Handlungsverlauf in Film und Roman**. Die Nummerierungen hinter den einzelnen Kapiteln zeigen an, für welche Themenbereiche in dieser Unterrichtseinheit die Episo-den vorgesehen sind. Natürlich ergeben sich darüber hinaus weitere Möglichkeiten zum Einsatz des Films im Unterricht. Zur optimalen Abstimmung auf den individuel-len Unterricht lassen sich inhaltliche Überschneidungen zwischen Roman und Verfil-mung mithilfe der Grafiken aber leicht feststellen.

Q & A

Aufbau von Film und Roman

Epilogue (6 Monate später): Ram und Nita als Ehepaar ⑥

1,000,000,000 **The Thirteenth Question:** Ram als Gewinner der Show ⑦

100,000,000 **X Gkrz Opknu:** Fremdenführer in **Agra**, Treffen mit Nita, arrangierte Ehen ⑥ ⑦ ⑧

10,000,000 **Tragedy Queen:** Ram als Dienstbote von Neelima Kumari in **Mumbai** ② ③ ⑤

1,000,000 **Licence to Kill:** Rams Rückkehr nach **Mumbai**, Salim bei Killer Ahmed Khan

500,000 **A Soldier's Tale:** Geschichte vom Krieg zwischen Indien und Pakistan (**Mumbai**)

200,000 **Murder on the Western Express:** Überfall auf Zugfahrt nach **Agra** ⑧

100,000 **Hold on to your Buttons:** Kellner in **Mumbai**, Geschichte der Voodoopriesterin ③ ⑧

50,000 **How to Speak Australian:** Diener für den australischen Botschafter Taylor in **Delhi**

10,000 **A Thought for the Crippled:** Waisenhaus in **Delhi**, Bettlercamp in **Mumbai**, Flucht ③ ④ ⑧

5,000 **A Brother's Promise:** Ram als Beschützer von Gudiya Shantaram in **Mumbai** ③ ⑧

2,000 **The Burden of a Priest:** Adoption Rams, Leben bei Father Timothy in **Delhi** ②

1,000 **Death of a Hero:** Armaan Ali als Bollywood-Idol von Rams Freund Salim (**Mumbai**) ⑤

Prologue: Rams Verhaftung und Verhör durch die Polizei in **Mumbai**

Slumdog Millionaire

Kapitel 11   Wiedersehen von Jamal und Latika, Happy End

Kapitel 10   Freilassung von Jamal, Kontakt mit Latika, Gewinn der Quizshow, Tod von Salim

Kapitel 9   Vereitelung von Latikas und Jamals Treffen durch Salim

Kapitel 8   Jamals Wiedersehen mit Latika und Salim, beide in Diensten bei Gangsterboss Javed Khan

Kapitel 7   Verschwinden von Salim und Latika, Jamals Arbeit als *chai wallah* in einem Callcenter

Kapitel 6   Befreiung von Latika in **Mumbai**, Ermordung von Maman durch Salim

Kapitel 5   Fahrt nach **Agra** ohne Latika, Jamal und Salim als Fremdenführer ⑧

Kapitel 4   Jamal, Salim und Latika im Bettlercamp von Maman, Flucht aus dem Waisenhaus ⑨

Kapitel 3   Rassenunruhen im Slum, Tod von Jamals Mutter durch fanatische Hindus

Kapitel 2   Jamals Kampf um ein Autogramm von Filmstar Amitabh Bachchan

Kapitel 1   Jamal K. Maliks Verhaftung und Folter durch die Polizei in **Mumbai**,
Rückblende auf Jamals Kindheit im Slum mit seinem Bruder Salim ①

Methodik/ Didaktik Im Mittelpunkt der Sequenz steht die Interpretation thematischer Schwerpunkte des Romans. Die verschiedenen Aspekte der indischen Kultur, Lebensweise und Gesellschaft werden romanimmanent beleuchtet, gedeutet und anschließend mithilfe verschiedener Sachtexte in ihrer Relevanz für die indische Gesellschaft betrachtet. Dadurch können interkulturelles Lernen, landeskundliche Inhalte sowie Literaturarbeit miteinander verknüpft werden. Die Unterrichtseinheit zeichnet sich insbesondere durch ihre **Handlungs- und Problemorientierung** aus. Aufbauend auf den Erkenntnissen aus der Arbeit mit Roman und Film nehmen die Schüler die **Perspektive der handelnden Personen** ein, beurteilen kritisch deren Entscheidungen und werden so Teil der Lebenswelt der Protagonisten.

Es ist gerade die Verzahnung der unterschiedlichen inhaltlichen Gesichtspunkte, die letztlich ein **facettenreiches Gesamtbild des Subkontinents** ergibt. Die Mannigfaltigkeit der gesammelten Eindrücke wird den Schülern nochmals vor Augen geführt, wenn sie zum Abschluss der Unterrichtseinheit die für sie interessantesten Aspekte zum Thema Indien auf Puzzleteile schreiben, die sie anschließend zu einer Indien-Karte (KV 9.2) zusammensetzen können.

Der Roman wird im Vorfeld der Einheit von den Schülern zu Hause gelesen. Diese Vorgehensweise ermöglicht es, sich kapitelübergreifend im Roman zu bewegen und Themen in ihrer Entwicklung im Roman zu erarbeiten. Die **Themenbereiche 2–8** haben modulartigen Charakter und können **in beliebiger Reihenfolge** behandelt werden. Je nach zur Verfügung stehender Zeit können auch nur einzelne Themen herausgegriffen werden. Es empfiehlt sich jedoch, den Themenbereich 1 „Stories within a Story" zu Beginn der Sequenz zu stellen, da die Schüler so einen Überblick über die Verzahnung von Rahmen- und Binnenhandlung im Roman gewinnen. Der Themenbereich 9 „*Q & A* on Screen – *Slumdog Millionaire*" sollte dagegen am Ende der Einheit stehen, da er auf den Eindrücken aufbaut, die während der Auseinandersetzung mit Roman und Film gesammelt wurden.

Medien Textgrundlage:
Vikas Swarup: *Q & A.* London (Black Swan), 2006.

Filme:
Danny Boyle, Loveleen Tandan (Regie): *Slumdog Millionaire*. Celeador Films 2009.
Amol Palekar (Regie): *Paheli.* Red Chillies Entertainment 2005.

Videoclip *(auf der beiliegenden CD-ROM vorhanden)*:
Photography: Sean Harder and Amy Bakke. Videography and Post-Production: Christina Mac Gillivray. Narration: Keith Porter. Script Writing: Sean Harder and Christina Mac Gillivray. © The Stanley Foundation

MP3-Datei *(auf der beiliegenden CD-ROM vorhanden)*:
© bononiasound/iStockphoto

Themenbereiche • Methodisch-didaktische Hinweise

1 Stories within a Story

> **Zeitbedarf:** ca. eine Unterrichtsstunde
>
> **Kompetenzen:**
> - Durchschauen der Struktur des Romans
> - Herstellen eines Bezugs zwischen Roman und Film
>
> **Material:** KV 1
>
> **Lektüre:**
> - vorbereitend: gesamter Roman
> - während der Erarbeitung: S. 369/370 (Frage 3 des Interviews mit Vikas Swarup)
>
> **Medien:**
> - Film *Slumdog Millionaire* (vgl. Einführung), Filmbeginn bis Min. 00:05:21

Dieser Themenbereich, der sich mit der **Erarbeitung der Romanstruktur** beschäftigt, empfiehlt sich für den Einstieg in die Arbeit mit *Q & A*. Die Lektüre sollten die Schüler im Vorfeld zu Hause gelesen haben, da es für die weitere Auseinandersetzung wichtig ist, das **Zusammenspiel von Rahmen- und Binnenhandlung** zu durchschauen.

Zu Beginn erhalten sie die Möglichkeit, sich über Verständnisprobleme und Interessens- → KV 1
gebiete auszutauschen. Diese **Rückmeldungen** können auch für den Lehrer aufschlussreich sein, um den Unterricht optimal an die Bedürfnisse der Schüler anzupassen und entsprechende Schwerpunkte zu setzen.

Als Einstieg in die Erarbeitung der Romanstruktur dient die **erste Szene der Verfil-** →
mung *Slumdog Millionaire* (Jamals Verhör und Beginn der Quizshow – Jamal K. Malik → KV 1
ist die Filmversion des Protagonisten Ram im Roman; Filmbeginn bis Min. 00:05:21).
Die Schüler ordnen diese Szene in den Gesamtkontext des Romans ein und sortieren daraufhin die einzelnen **Episoden von Q&A in chronologischer Reihenfolge.** Diese werden schließlich mit der Abfolge der Filmkapitel verglichen, um ein besseres Verständnis für das Prinzip von Rahmen- und Binnenhandlung zu schaffen, das dem Roman zugrunde liegt. Um offene Fragen sofort beantworten zu können, empfiehlt es sich, einen Schüler die Arbeitsergebnisse vorstellen zu lassen (Prinzip des *five-minute teacher*) und diese dann gemeinsam auszuwerten und einer tiefer gehenden Betrachtung zu unterziehen. Anschließend lesen die Schüler einen Abschnitt aus dem Interview mit Romanautor Vikas Swarup im Anhang der Romanausgabe, um zu klären, warum dieser komplizierte Aufbau für die Handlung gewählt wurde.

2 One Country – Many Religions

> **!**
>
> **Zeitbedarf:** ca. eine Unterrichtsstunde
>
> **Kompetenzen:**
> - Herstellen von Bezügen zwischen fiktionaler und realer Welt hinsichtlich des Zusammenlebens der unterschiedlichen Religionen in Indien
> - selbstständige Internetrecherche
> - Verfassen eines Tagebucheintrags aus der Perspektive des Protagonisten
>
> **Material:** KV 2
>
> **Lektüre:**
> - während der Erarbeitung: S. 50–55, 94/95, 244/245
>
> **Medien:**
> - Computer, Internet
> - Wörterbücher

→ KV 2 Die verschiedenen **Religionen Indiens** und der **Umgang der Gesellschaft mit die-**
→ 🖥 **ser Vielfalt** stehen nun im Fokus. Zunächst werden die Schüler affektiv auf das Thema eingestimmt, indem sie per (Internet-)Recherche Informationen über die **Herkunft und Bedeutung ihrer Namen** zusammentragen. Hierbei bietet es sich an, verschiedene Nationalitäten (falls in der Lerngruppe vorhanden) zu Wort kommen zu lassen, um die Diversität in der Lebenswelt und Religion der Schüler hervorzuheben. Zur besseren Anschaulichkeit empfiehlt es sich, die Namen an der Tafel zu sammeln und den einzelnen Religionen zuzuordnen. Analog zu den Schülernamen wird auch der Name des Protagonisten untersucht und so die Verbindung zum Roman geschaffen.

→ KV 2 Anschließend analysieren die Schüler die Haltung des Protagonisten zu den unterschiedlichen Religionen Indiens mithilfe geeigneter Romanpassagen und **hinterfragen** anhand eines Sachtextes kritisch **die Beziehung der Religionen zueinander**. Hierfür sollten, wie generell für die Arbeit mit unbekannten Texten in dieser Unterrichtseinheit, Wörterbücher zur Verfügung stehen. Die fiktive Welt des Romans und die Realität in Indien werden abschließend verglichen, indem die Schüler eine Bewertung des im Roman beschriebenen *All Faith Committee* vornehmen.

Zur Abrundung des Themenbereichs reflektieren die Schüler die Bedeutung von Reli-
→ KV 2 gionszugehörigkeit für das alltägliche Leben in Indien, indem sie einen **Tagebuchein-trag** aus Rams Perspektive verfassen. Danach verschaffen sich die Schüler, beispielsweise im *milling around*-Verfahren, einen Eindruck von den Werken ihrer Klassenkameraden. Auf einem leeren Blatt neben dem jeweiligen Tagebucheintrag können Bewertungen der Aufgabe vorgenommen werden, wobei zwei unterschiedliche Farben für Lob und konstruktive Kritik bereitliegen sollten.

3 Housing in Big Indian Cities

!

Zeitbedarf: ca. zwei Unterrichtsstunden/eine Doppelstunde

Kompetenzen:

- Analyse und Bewertung von Wohnsituationen in Indien
- Anstellen von Vergleichen zwischen Realität und Roman hinsichtlich der Darstellung der Wohnsituation in Indien
- Diskussion zur Situation sozial schwacher Familien in Indien und Deutschland

Material: KV 3.1/KV 3.2, Farbfolie oder farbige Version (KV 3.1) von CD-ROM, Videoclip „Dharavi" (auf beiliegender CD-ROM vorhanden)

Lektüre:

- während der Erarbeitung: S. 70–84, 156/157, 245–247, 268

Medien:

- Computer, Beamer

Der Themenbereich behandelt die verschiedenen Lebens- und Wohnbedingungen in indischen Großstädten. Zur Einstimmung werden als visueller Impuls je zwei **Bilder zu** → KV 3.1
den drei verschiedenen **Wohnsituationen** (in Slums, Chawls und Luxusapartments) → Farbfolie
präsentiert, die von den Schülern kategorisiert und beschrieben werden.
An die Bildanalyse schließt sich die Erarbeitung der **Vor- und Nachteile des Lebens** → KV 3.1
im Slum, Chawl oder Luxusviertel an. Zunächst wird ein kurzes **Video** über die Le- →
bensrealität in Dharavi, dem größten Slum Mumbais ausgewertet. Da sich die Situation
in Dharavi momentan sehr schnell entwickelt, bietet es sich an, die Schüler zusätzlich
in Partnerarbeit in einer kurzen **Internetrecherche** Informationen zum aktuellen →
Stand der Dinge zusammentragen zu lassen. Danach wird der Sachtext „Life in a Chawl"
von den Schülern analysiert. Die beiden Quellen vermitteln realistische Einblicke in das
Alltagsleben in der Megastadt Mumbai. Die Ergebnisse der Quellenarbeit sollten anschließend gemeinsam gesichert werden, sodass die Schüler über ein einheitliches Hin-
tergrundwissen verfügen, bevor sie im *think-pair-share*-Verfahren anhand von Aus-
zügen die Darstellung der unterschiedlichen Lebenswelten im Roman erarbeiten und
dann einen kritischen Vergleich zwischen Lektüre und Realität ziehen.
Eine Textproduktion leitet zu einem neuen Aspekt des Themenbereichs über. Anhand
einer Textpassage aus *Q & A* verfassen die Schüler einen **Bericht zum sozialen Ab-** → KV 3.2
stieg einer indischen Familie. An die exemplarische Besprechung der Texte schließt sich
ein Vergleich mit der Situation von sozial schlecht gestellten Familien in Deutschland
an. Diese Ideensammlung kann in Form eines *brainstorming* erfolgen, in dem die wich-
tigsten Aspekte an der Tafel notiert werden. Dies ist vor allem für die Vorbereitung des
folgenden **Rollenspiels** von Vorteil, für das die Schüler in Gruppen Argumente vorbe- → KV 3.2
reiten. Es ist empfehlenswert, die Diskussion nach dem *fishbowl*-Prinzip durchzufüh-
ren, da dann die Rollen der Diskussionsteilnehmer immer wieder von neuen Schülern
besetzt werden und so ein reger Gedankenaustausch möglich wird.

4   Orphans in India

> **Zeitbedarf:** ca. eine Unterrichtsstunde
>
> **Kompetenzen:**
> - Sammeln und Vergleichen von Informationen zu den tatsächlichen Verhältnissen in indischen Waisenhäusern
> - Verfassen eines formellen Briefs
> - Geben von differenzierten Rückmeldungen innerhalb der *peer group*
>
> **Material:** KV 4
>
> **Lektüre:**
> - während der Erarbeitung: S. 91–93, 96/97, 100/101, 108, 117
>
> **Medien:**
> - Plakate
> - Computer, Internet
> - Wörterbücher

→ KV 4

→ Plakate

Dieser Themenbereich ist den **Lebensbedingungen der Waisenkinder in Indien** gewidmet. Die Schüler erhalten mittels eines **stummen visuellen Impulses** einen affektiven Zugang zu der Thematik. Anhand von geeigneten Passagen des Romans analysieren sie die Darstellung zweier Waisenhäuser und schließen sich dann zu Gruppen zusammen, um ihre Erkenntnisse auf Plakaten festzuhalten. Gemeinsam kann im Anschluss das Plakat gewählt werden, dass die Informationen am prägnantesten präsentiert.

→ KV 4
→ 🖳

Durch die Bearbeitung eines kurzen Sachtextes verschaffen sich die Schüler Einblick in die Ursachen für die steigende Anzahl verwaister Kinder. Per **Internetrecherche** informieren sie sich über die generellen Bedingungen in indischen Waisenhäusern. Abschließend findet ein gemeinsamer Vergleich der Darstellung in Roman und Realität statt.

→ KV 4

Der Themenbereich wird abgerundet, indem der Bogen zurück zum Roman geschlossen wird. Die Schüler verfassen einen **offenen Brief** aus Rams Perspektive, der seine Popularität als Millionengewinner nutzt, um die indische Öffentlichkeit auf die schrecklichen Zustände in den Waisenhäusern aufmerksam zu machen. Die Bewertung der einzelnen Arbeiten nehmen die Schüler selbst in Dreiergruppen vor. Jeder Brief wird gele-

→ KV 4

sen und anhand eines **Evaluationsbogens** beurteilt. Um einen größtmöglichen Lerneffekt zu erzielen, bietet es sich an, die Schüler ihre Produkte anhand des Bewertungsbogens verbessern zu lassen und die Endversion danach zur Korrektur einzusammeln.

5 Bollywood and its Function for Indian People

> **Zeitbedarf:** ca. eine Unterrichtsstunde
>
> **Kompetenzen:**
> - Kennenlernen charakteristischer Merkmale von Bollywood-Filmen
> - Verstehen von deren Funktion und Bedeutung für die indische Bevölkerung
> - Kritische Reflexion des Kontrasts zwischen der Filmwelt und den harten Lebensbedingungen der einfachen Bevölkerung
>
> **Material:** KV 5
>
> **Lektüre:**
> - während der Erarbeitung: S. 31–35, 246/247, 250/251, 253, 260, 267
>
> **Medien:**
> - Film *Paheli* (vgl. Einführung), Min. 1:05:57–1:08:40
> - Wörterbücher
> - Placemats (in DIN A3-Format)

Der Fokus dieses Themenbereichs liegt auf den **Bollywood-Filmen**, die in Deutschland auch immer populärer werden. Mit der Frage nach ihren **Lieblingsstars aus Hollywood** werden die Schüler an das Thema „Filme und Stars" herangeführt. Ein Filmplakat und ein kurzer **Ausschnitt aus dem Film** *Paheli* (Tanz mit den Armreifen, Min. 1:05:57–1:08:40) bringen den Schülern im Vergleich dazu die Welt von Bollywood näher und schaffen eine affektive Basis. → KV 5

Im weiteren Verlauf beschäftigen sich die Schüler in Gruppen mit der **Rolle Bollywoods für die Menschen in Indien**. Sie betrachten dafür sowohl die fiktive Welt verschiedener Romancharaktere als auch die Realität, wie sie in einem Sachtext dargestellt wird. Gemeinsam sollen die Schüler dann zusammentragen, welche Rolle Bollywood für Inder spielt. Hierfür empfiehlt sich die **Placemat-Methode**, um die Ergebnisse festzuhalten. Aufbauend auf den Erkenntnissen der *placemat activity* äußern die Schüler im Blitzlicht-Verfahren ihre Vermutungen, weshalb der Autor die Bollywood-Schauspielerin Neelima Kumari Selbstmord begehen lässt. → KV 5

Abschließend setzen die Schüler die in der Analyse gewonnenen Erkenntnisse kreativ um und schreiben aus der Perspektive der Schauspielerin Neelima einen **Abschiedsbrief**. Die Besprechung der Texte kann beispielsweise zunächst in Vierergruppen in Form einer *peer evaluation* erfolgen. Nachdem jeder Schüler die Texte der Mitschüler gelesen hat, wird der beste Abschiedsbrief bestimmt und gemeinsam an Inhalt, Struktur und Sprache gefeilt. Anschließend präsentiert jede Gruppe ihren Text. → KV 5

6 Women in India

> **!**
>
> **Zeitbedarf:** ca. zwei Unterrichtsstunden/eine Doppelstunde
>
> **Kompetenzen:**
> - Verstehen der Chancenungleichheit zwischen Jungen und Mädchen in Indien
> - Durchführen einer Internetrecherche und kritische Analyse der Ergebnisse
> - Umsetzen eines handlungsorientierten Schreibauftrags
>
> **Material:** KV 6.1 / KV 6.2
>
> **Lektüre:**
> - während der Erarbeitung: S. 299–302, 304–306, 360
>
> **Medien:**
> - Internet
> - Computer, Beamer, Plakate

Der Themenkomplex beschäftigt sich sowohl mit dem **Alltag der Frauen in Indien** als auch mit den **Aktivitäten von Hilfsorganisationen**, die sich für diese Klientel einsetzen. Um einen affektiven Zugang zu der Thematik zu schaffen, nehmen zunächst nur die Schülerinnen dazu Stellung, was ihnen für ihre Zukunft besonders wichtig ist.

→ KV 6.1 Dies kann beispielsweise in Form eines **stummen Schreibgesprächs** erfolgen. Diese Methode hat den Vorteil, dass männliche Schüler an der lautlosen Kommunikation beteiligt werden können, indem sie Fragen zu den Antworten der Schülerinnen stellen oder diese kommentieren können. Anschließend werden Vergleiche zu der Situation der Mädchen in Indien gezogen.

Danach wird der Bogen zum **Roman** geschlagen: Die Schüler erarbeiten anhand rele-
→ KV 6.1 vanter Passagen in Stillarbeit die Situation von Rams zukünftiger Frau Nita und lesen zudem zwei Texte zur Lage von Frauen in Indien. Auf der Basis der gesammelten Erkenntnisse vollziehen sie in Partnerarbeit den **Teufelskreis** nach, **in dem viele Inderinnen gefangen sind**. Es bietet sich hier an, die Ergebnisse mit einem anderen Schülerpaar vergleichen zu lassen, um die Umsetzung im Schaubild selbstständig zu überprüfen. Abschließend vergleichen die Schüler die Situation der Frauen in den Sachtexten mit der der beiden Frauenfiguren im Roman, Nita und Gudiya Shantaram.

Die Überlegung, wie der Teufelskreis durchbrochen werden kann, leitet über zum zweiten Aspekt dieses Themenkomplexes, den **Hilfsorganisationen**. Die Schüler recher-
→ chieren paarweise im **Internet** nach Organisationen, die sich für die Verbesserung der
→ KV 6.2 Rechte und Chancen indischer Mädchen einsetzen, und präsentieren ihre Ergebnisse (auf Plakaten bzw. als Powerpoint-Präsentation) danach im Plenum. Die Mitschüler geben den Referenten anschließend mithilfe eines Bewertungsrasters Feedback. Ein Vergleich der unterschiedlichen Organisationen leitet zum kreativen Umgang mit den erlangten Erkenntnissen über.

→ Im Rahmen der Binnendifferenzierung wählen die Schüler zwischen **zwei handlungs-**
→ KV 6.2 **orientierten Schreibaufgaben** aus (einer E-Mail Rams an eine der vorgestellten Hilfsorganisationen, die er um Hilfe für Nita bittet, bzw. einem Dialog zwischen der mittlerweile mit Ram verheirateten Nita und einer fiktiven Freundin). Exemplarisch werden anschließend einige E-Mails vorgelesen und Dialoge vorgespielt.

→ KV 6.2 Zuletzt richten die Schüler ihren Blick wieder auf den Roman und analysieren die **Symbolik** hinter Nitas nicht vorhandenem **Nachnamen**.

7 Arranged Marriages

> **!**
>
> **Zeitbedarf:** ca. zwei Unterrichtsstunden/eine Doppelstunde
>
> **Kompetenzen:**
> - Differenzierte Betrachtung des fremden Konzepts der arrangierten Ehe
> - Vertreten einer vorgegebenen Meinung in einer Talkshow
> - Umsetzen der Erkenntnisse in einer kreativen Schreibaufgabe
>
> **Material:** KV 7
>
> **Lektüre:**
> - während der Erarbeitung: S. 292–294, 309/310, 313–315
>
> **Medien:**
> - Wörterbücher
> - Plakat

Der Fokus des Themenbereichs liegt auf den **arrangierten Ehen**, welche in Indien nach wie vor ein gängiges Konzept darstellen. Mittels Heiratsanzeigen aus der *Tribune India* werden die Schüler an das Thema herangeführt. Anschließend wird ein erstes Stimmungsbild zu arrangierten Ehen eingeholt. Hierfür empfiehlt sich die Methode der **Positionslinie**, denn wenn die Schüler sich entlang einer gedachten Linie zwischen zwei Extrempositionen aufstellen, lassen sich die unterschiedlichen Meinungen sehr anschaulich präsentieren. Danach können einige Schüler gebeten werden, sich zu den Gründen für ihre Haltung zu äußern. → KV 7

Daraufhin erarbeiten die Schüler arbeitsteilig die unterschiedlichen Positionen zu „arranged marriages". Für diesen Arbeitsauftrag eignet sich die Methode **Expertenpuzzle** besonders gut. Gemeinsam werden die Ergebnisse diskutiert und gesichert. Danach bewerten die Schüler Swarups Darstellung des Konzepts arrangierter Ehen im Roman. → KV 7

Aufbauend auf den Erkenntnissen des Expertenpuzzles wird eine **Talkshow** durchgeführt. Mithilfe von *role cards* bereiten die Schüler den Standpunkt ihres Charakters vor. Es bietet sich an, diese Vorbereitungsphase in Gruppen durchführen zu lassen und dann für die Talkshow jeweils einen Vertreter jeder Gruppe nach vorne zu bitten. Die Rolle des Showmasters sollte hierbei von einem leistungsstarken Schüler übernommen werden, da dieser neben der Befragung der Gäste auch das Publikum in die Show einbeziehen muss. Danach wird mittels einer **erneuten Positionslinie** überprüft, inwieweit die differenzierte Behandlung des Themas die Haltung der Schüler zu arrangierten Ehen beeinflusst hat. → KV 7   →

Abschließend verfassen die Schüler eine **Heiratsanzeige**, wie sie Rams Freundin Lajwanti für ihre Schwester aufgegeben haben könnte. Um eine komplette Seite aus dem Kleinanzeigenteil einer indischen Zeitung darzustellen, können die Anzeigen der Schüler auf einem größeren Plakat aufgeklebt und bei Bedarf gemeinsam besprochen werden. → KV 7   → Plakat

8   Tourism and Travelling in India

> **!**
>
> **Zeitbedarf:** ca. eine Unterrichtsstunde
>
> **Kompetenzen:**
> - Entwickeln eines affektiven Interesses am Reiseziel Indien
> - Vergleich der deutschen mit den indischen Reisegepflogenheiten anhand von Statistiken
> - Entwicklung kultureller Kompetenzen in Abgrenzung zu den negativ dargestellten deutschen Touristen im Roman
>
> **Material:** KV 8
>
> **Lektüre:**
> - während der Erarbeitung: S. 84–86, 91, 103/104, 155/156, 173/174, 190/191, 277–282, 294–297
>
> **Medien:**
> - MP3-Datei „Bollywood" (auf beiliegender CD-ROM vorhanden)
> - Film *Slumdog Millionaire*, Min. 00:36:00 – 00:39:00

Der Themenbereich widmet sich sowohl den **Reisegewohnheiten der Inder als auch der Indien-Touristen**. Um die Schüler mental durch Indien reisen zu lassen, wird zu
→ 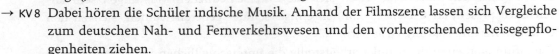 Beginn der Stunde ein Ausschnitt aus der Verfilmung *Slumdog Millionaire* ohne Ton gezeigt (Jamals und Salims Reise mit dem Zug durch Indien; Min. 00:36:00 – 00:39:00).

→ KV 8 Dabei hören die Schüler indische Musik. Anhand der Filmszene lassen sich Vergleiche zum deutschen Nah- und Fernverkehrswesen und den vorherrschenden Reisegepflogenheiten ziehen.

→ KV 8 Daran schließt sich die genauere Untersuchung der relevanten Romanpassagen in **ar-**
→ 👥 **beitsteiliger Gruppenarbeit** an. Im Sinne der Binnendifferenzierung kann den Schülern hier freigestellt werden, welche der Aufgaben sie lieber bearbeiten möchten, da die Ergebnisse anschließend gemeinsam besprochen werden. In einem weiteren Schritt erarbeiten die Schüler mithilfe diverser Statistiken die **Unterschiede im Reiseverhalten von Indern und westlichen Urlaubern**.

→ KV 8 In einem abrundenden Unterrichtsgespräch reflektieren die Schüler Swarups Absichten hinsichtlich der Darstellung der Touristen in Agra. Die Meinung der Schüler kann beispielsweise in Form eines **Blitzlichts** eingeholt werden. Abschließend überlegen sich die Schüler, ob sie selbst gerne nach Indien reisen würden, und begründen ihre Entscheidung.

9 Q&A on Screen – *Slumdog Millionaire*

!

Zeitbedarf: ca. zwei Unterrichtsstunden/eine Doppelstunde

Kompetenzen:
- Analyse der spezifischen Möglichkeiten der Medien Film und Roman
- Auseinandersetzung mit konträren Standpunkten
- Differenzierte Bewertung von Roman und Film

Material: KV 9.1 / KV 9.2

Lektüre:
- während der Erarbeitung: S. 108, 116–119

Medien:
- Film *Slumdog Millionaire*, Min. 00:21:48–00:34:10
- Wörterbücher

Die Verfilmung von *Q & A* **sowie deren Rezeption in der** indischen und westlichen **Öffentlichkeit** steht nun im Mittelpunkt: *Slumdog Millionaire* erschien 2008 und wurde 2009 mit acht Oscars ausgezeichnet, darunter als „bester Film" und „bestes adaptiertes Drehbuch".

Als Einstieg dient eine Stoffsammlung zu den Vor- und Nachteilen der Medien Roman → KV 9.1 und Film. So sollen die Schüler für den folgenden **Vergleich einer Szene aus Roman und Film** (Jamals und Salims Flucht aus dem „home for the crippled", Min. 00:21:48– → 🎞️ 00:34:10) sensibilisiert werden und ihren Blick auf die jeweiligen Darstellungsmöglichkeiten schärfen. Im Anschluss werden die Effekte besprochen, die durch die Veränderungen in der Filmversion gegenüber der Romanhandlung erzielt werden.

Daran schließt sich eine Sachtextanalyse an, in der die Schüler sich mit den Reaktionen → KV 9.1 auf den Film auseinandersetzen. Unter Rückgriff auf die gesehene Filmszene sollen die Schüler dann weitere **mögliche Kritikpunkte der indischen Öffentlichkeit** anführen und deren Stichhaltigkeit bewerten. Zuletzt schreiben die Schüler eine abrundende **Bewertung des Romans Q&A** und gehen darin darauf ein, ob er als Grundlage für eine Beschäftigung mit dem Thema Indien geeignet ist.

Zum Abschluss der Einheit können die Schüler zehn Aspekte, die ihnen im Zusammen- → KV 9.2 hang mit Indien am interessantesten erscheinen, auf einzelne Puzzleteile schreiben und diese dann zu ihrer persönlichen **Indienkarte** zusammensetzen.

Am Ende der Unterrichtseinheit kann eine **Klausur** gestellt werden. → KV 10

Vorschlag zur Stoffverteilung

		Thema der Stunde und Unterrichtsverlauf	Unterrichtsmittel
1. Stunde	**1**	**Stories within a Story**	
		Einstieg: Sammeln der ersten Eindrücke zum Roman, Thematisieren von Verständnisproblemen *(Einzelarbeit, Plenum)*	→ KV 1
		Erarbeitung: Präsentation der Anfangsszene von *Slumdog Millionaire*, Einordnen der Ereignisse in den Gesamtkontext des Romans *(Plenum)*	→ Film
		Vertiefung: Ordnen von Romanschauplätzen und -handlungen in chronologischer Reihenfolge sowie nach der Behandlung im Roman *(Partnerarbeit, five-minute teacher)*, Analyse der Erzählstruktur *(Unterrichtsgespräch)*, Beschäftigung mit der Romanstruktur anhand eines Interviews mit dem Autor	→ KV 1, Lektüre
		Hausaufgabe: Internetrecherche zur Herkunft und Bedeutung der Namen der Schüler	→ KV 2, Internet
2. Stunde	**2**	**One Country – Many Religions**	
		Einstieg: Reflektieren der Namen der Schüler und deren kultureller Hintergründe *(Unterrichtsgespräch)*	→ KV 2
		Erarbeitung: Analyse der drei Namen Rams und deren Verwendung *(Einzelarbeit, Plenum)*, Kennenlernen und kritisches Hinterfragen der *anti-conversion laws* in Rajasthan *(Partnerarbeit, Plenum)*	→ KV 2, Lektüre Wörterbücher
		Vertiefung: Bewertung des *All Faith Committee* im Roman *(Plenum)*, Vergleich der geschilderten Beziehung der Religionen zueinander im Roman und im Sachtext *(Plenum)*	→ KV 2
		Hausaufgabe: Verfassen eines Tagebucheintrags der Romanfigur Ram im Spannungsfeld der Religionen *(Einzelarbeit)*	→ KV 2
3./4. Stunde	**3**	**Housing in Big Indian Cities**	
		Besprechung der Hausaufgabe: Bewertung der Tagebucheinträge in Form der *peer evaluation (milling around)*	→ KV 2
		Einstieg: Assoziationen zu Bildern verschiedener Wohnsituationen in Indien *(Unterrichtsgespräch)*	→ KV 3.1, Farbfolie
		Erarbeitung: Auswerten eines Videos über das Slum Dharavi *(Einzelarbeit)*, Recherche der aktuellen Situation in Dharavi im Internet *(Partnerarbeit)*, Beleuchten der Lebensumstände in einem *chawl* anhand eines Sachtextes *(Partnerarbeit, Plenum)*	→ Videoclip „Dharavi", Internet, KV 3.1
		Vertiefung: Aufzeigen von Vor- und Nachteilen der verschiedenen Lebenssituationen im Roman *(think-pair-share)*, Vergleich der Darstellung der Lebenssituationen in Video, Roman und Sachtext *(Unterrichtsgespräch)*	→ KV 3.1, Lektüre
		Erarbeitung: Bericht über den sozialen Abstieg der Familie Shantaram *(Einzelarbeit)*, Vergleich mit ähnlichen Situationen in Deutschland *(brainstorming)*	→ KV 3.2, Lektüre
		Transfer: Rollenspiel zur Gegenüberstellung der Sozialsysteme Deutschlands und Indiens *(fishbowl discussion)*	→ KV 3.2

5. Stunde	**4**	**Orphans in India**	
		Einstieg: Assoziationen zu einem Bildimpuls *(Unterrichtsgespräch)*	→ KV 4
		Erarbeitung: Zusammenfassung von Rams Erfahrungen in den beiden Waisenhäusern *(Einzelarbeit)*, Entwerfen und Präsentieren von Plakaten *(Gruppenarbeit, Plenum)*	→ KV 4, Lektüre → Plakate
		Vertiefung: Erarbeiten von Hintergrundinformationen zur Situation der Waisen in Indien anhand eines Sachtextes und per Internetrecherche *(Partnerarbeit)*, Bewertung der Realitätsnähe der Romanhandlung *(Unterrichtsgespräch)*	→ KV 4, Wörterbücher, Internet
		Transfer: Verfassen eines Briefs aus Rams Perspektive *(Einzelarbeit)*, Rückmeldung über *peer evaluation* durch die Mitschüler *(Gruppenarbeit)*	→ KV 4
		Hausaufgabe: Überarbeiten des eigenen Briefs anhand der Evaluationsbögen	→ KV 4
6. Stunde	**5**	**Bollywood and its Function for Indian People**	
		Besprechung der Hausaufgabe: Einsammeln der Schülerarbeiten und Korrektur durch die Lehrkraft *(Plenum)*	
		Einstieg: Sprechen über die Lieblings-Hollywoodstars der Schüler, Interpretieren eines Bollywood-Filmplakats *(Unterrichtsgespräch)*, Präsentation und Analyse einer Szene aus dem Bollywood-Film *Paheli* *(Stillarbeit, Plenum)*	→ KV 5 → Film *Paheli*
		Erarbeitung: Herausarbeiten der Funktion Bollywoods für diverse Romanfiguren und die Inder im realen Leben *(placemat activity, Plenum)*	→ KV 5, Lektüre, Wörterbücher
		Vertiefung: Diskussion über den Selbstmord der Bollywood-Schauspielerin Neelima Kumari im Roman *(Blitzlicht, Unterrichtsgespräch)*	→ KV 5
		Hausaufgabe: Verfassen des Abschiedsbriefs von Neelima Kumari	→ KV 5
7./8. Stunde	**6**	**Women in India**	
		Besprechung der Hausaufgabe: Rückmeldung zu den Abschiedsbriefen über *peer evaluation* durch die Mitschüler, weitere Bearbeitung und Vortragen der besten Lösung *(Gruppenarbeit, Plenum)*	→ KV 5
		Einstieg: Sammeln von Wünschen und Zukunftsplänen der Schülerinnen *(stummes Schreibgespräch)*, Vergleich der Situation deutscher Mädchen mit der der Inderinnen *(Unterrichtsgespräch)*	→ KV 6.1
		Erarbeitung: Untersuchung der Lage von Rams Freundin Nita *(Einzelarbeit)*, Erarbeiten des Teufelskreises, in dem sich viele indische Frauen befinden, anhand zweier Sachtexte *(Partnerarbeit, Gruppenarbeit)*, Vergleich von Realität und Fiktion hinsichtlich der Lebensbedingungen von Frauen in Indien *(Plenum)*	→ KV 6.1, Lektüre
		Vertiefung: Sammeln von Möglichkeiten, aus dem Teufelskreis auszubrechen *(Unterrichtsgespräch)*	→ KV 6.1
		Erarbeitung: Internetrecherche zu Hilfsorganisationen für Frauen in Indien *(Partnerarbeit)*, Präsentation der Ergebnisse *(Partnerarbeit, Plenum)*, Evaluation der Präsentationen durch Mitschüler	→ KV 6.2, Internet → Plakate, Beamer, Computer
		Vertiefung: Finden von Gemeinsamkeiten der Hilfsorganisationen *(Unterrichtsgespräch)*	→ KV 6.2
		Hausaufgabe: Verfassen eines Dialogs über die Situation der Frauen in Indien oder einer E-Mail Rams an eine der Hilfsorganisationen, Analyse der Bedeutung eines Nachnamens für Nita	→ KV 6.2 → Lektüre

9./10. Stunde	7	**Arranged Marriages**	
		Besprechung der Hausaufgabe: Vorführen der Dialoge, Besprechen einiger exemplarischer E-Mails, Klären der Bedeutung eines Nachnamens für Nita *(Plenum)*	→ KV 6.2
		Einstieg: Interpretieren von Heiratsanzeigen aus der *Tribune India (Unterrichtsgespräch)*, Darstellen des Stimmungsbildes zum Thema arrangierte Ehen in Form einer Positionslinie *(Plenum)*	→ KV 7
		Erarbeitung: Auseinandersetzung mit unterschiedlichen Sichtweisen zu arrangierten Ehen bzw. romanimmanente Analyse der Thematik *(arbeitsteilige Partnerarbeit, Expertenpuzzle)*, Bewertung der Darstellung im Roman *(Unterrichtsgespräch)*	→ KV 7, Lektüre, Wörterbücher
		Transfer: Vorbereitung und Durchführung einer Talkshow zum Thema *arranged marriages (Gruppenarbeit, Plenum)*	→ KV 7
		Vertiefung: erneute Stellungnahme der Schüler an der Positionslinie, Vergleich der Ergebnisse mit den vorherrschenden Meinungen zu Stundenbeginn *(Plenum)*	→ KV 7
		Hausaufgabe: Verfassen einer Heiratsanzeige für Lakshmi, die Schwester von Rams Freundin Lajwanti	→ KV 7
11. Stunde	**8**	**Tourism and Travelling in India**	
		Besprechung der Hausaufgabe: Erstellung einer Zeitungsseite aus der Rubrik *Classifieds (Plenum)*	→ Plakat
		Einstieg: Präsentation eines Ausschnitts aus dem Film *Slumdog Millionaire*, Vergleich der indischen Art des Reisens mit den deutschen Gepflogenheiten *(silent viewing, Unterrichtsgespräch)*	→ KV 8, Film, MP3-Datei „Bollywood"
		Erarbeitung: Nachverfolgen der Reisen Rams im Roman bzw. Analyse der Darstellung von Touristen in Indien aus Rams Sicht *(arbeitsteilige Gruppenarbeit, Plenum)*, Auswerten von Statistiken zum Tourismus in Indien *(Einzelarbeit, Plenum)*	→ KV 8, Lektüre
		Vertiefung: Finden einer Begründung für Swarups Darstellung von Touristen *(Blitzlicht, Unterrichtsgespräch)*	→ KV 8
		Hausaufgabe: Reflektieren des eigenen Interesses an einer Reise nach Indien	→ KV 8
12./13. Stunde	**9**	**Q & A on Screen – *Slumdog Millionaire***	
		Besprechung der Hausaufgabe: Sammeln und Auswerten der Argumente für und gegen eine Reise nach Indien *(Unterrichtsgespräch)*	→ KV 8
		Einstieg: allgemeine Gegenüberstellung der Medien Roman und Film *(Unterrichtsgespräch)*	→ KV 9.1
		Erarbeitung: Querlesen einer Romanszene *(Einzelarbeit)*, Analyse einer Filmszene aus *Slumdog Millionaire*, Vergleich mit der Romanvorlage *(Einzelarbeit, Plenum)*, Erarbeitung und kritisches Hinterfragen der unterschiedlichen Reaktionen auf den Film anhand eines Sachtextes *(Partnerarbeit, Plenum)*	→ Lektüre, Film → KV 9.1, Wörterbücher
		Evaluation: Verfassen einer Kritik zum Roman *Q & A (Einzelarbeit, Unterrichtsgespräch)*, Schaffen eines Überblicks über die interessantesten Themen der Unterrichtseinheit anhand einer Karte von Indien *(Einzelarbeit, Plenum)*	→ KV 9.1 → KV 9.2

Kopiervorlagen

| KV 1 | **Many Stories to Tell** |

First Impressions on *Q & A / Slumdog Millionaire*

1 We are going to collect your first impressions of the novel *Q & A*.

- Think about the following three questions on the novel. Then make notes on the cards below.
  You do not need to write full sentences.
  Keywords will be sufficient.

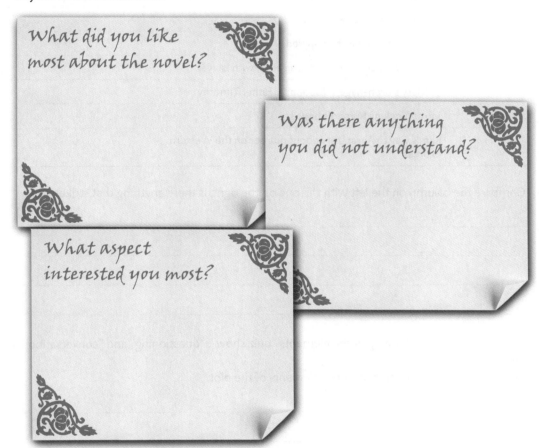

What did you like most about the novel?

Was there anything you did not understand?

What aspect interested you most?

- Read out your notes. If some of your ideas have already been mentioned, present only the new ones.

Stories within a Story – The Structure of *Q & A* and *Slumdog Millionaire*

2 Now that you have pointed out your reactions to the novel, let's jump right into the plot:

  a Watch the beginning of the film version *Slumdog Millionaire* and decide ...
  - when these situations take place according to the chronological order of events (i.e. the way in which Jamal – Ram's name in the film – experiences them, one after the other).
  - when all the events Jamal thinks about have happened.

  b Compare the film scene to *Q & A*. When are the events of the film scene presented in the novel?

3 Together with a partner, work with the novel and fill in the grid:
  • Put the events/sites in chronological order by writing the correct number in the left-hand column.
  • Put the events/sites in the correct order according to their presentation in the novel.
    Give the number of the quiz number and the name of the chapter in the right-hand column.

Chronological order	Plot/Setting in *Q&A*	Chapter (Number)
	Juvenile home in Delhi: Ram meets Salim	
	• Life in Dharavi, job at Jimmy's restaurant: story about Voodoo • Bumps into Salim: story called "licence to kill"	
	Job as a tourist guide in Agra	
	Mumbai, home for the crippled	
	Quiz show, questioning, conversation with lawyer	
	St Mary's orphanage, adoption by Father Timothy	
	Job at Neelima Kumari's house	
	Ram's way to Agra: story about murder on the Western express	

4 Compare the column on the left with the one on the right. Is there anything that strikes you?

_____

_____

_____

_____

5 Take a look at the positioning of the elements "quiz show", "questioning" and "conversation with the lawyer" in the novel.
Explain how far they differ from other elements of the plot.

_____

_____

_____

6 Turn to the additional material in the back of your novel and read Swarup's comment on the structure of his novel on pages 369 to 370 (question number 3 in the interview).
Briefly summarize why the author chose this complicated structure.

_____

_____

_____

_____

KV 2 **One Country – Many Religions**

1 Gather information from the internet (or ask your parents) in order to explain to your classmates …
- the origin of your name.
- if there is a famous person/saint you were named after.
- what religious belief your name derives from.

2 Now read the pages listed in brackets after the following tasks and write your answers down.

a Explain where Ram's full name, Ram Mohammad Thomas, comes from (cf. *Q & A*, pp. 50–53).

_____

_____

_____

_____

_____

b Assess the relations between the different religions in India as presented in the novel (cf. *Q & A*, pp. 94/95).

_____

_____

_____

_____

c Describe Ram's attitude towards religion (cf. *Q & A*, pp. 53–55).

_____

_____

_____

_____

d Explain how Ram Mohammad Thomas uses his name (cf. *Q & A*, p. 244/245).

_____

_____

_____

_____

_____

_____

"Black" Day for India: New Anti-Conversion Law in Rajasthan

Cardinal Varkey Vithayathil denounces to AsiaNews the uselessness of the decree. According to the text, those who convert by "use of force, allurement or fraudulent means" risk five years in prison.

1 Jaipur (AsiaNews) – After more than two years of parliamentary debate, the assembly of the western state of Rajasthan has approved a new anti-conversion law. Cardinal Varkey Vi-
5 thayathil, archbishop of Ernakulam-Angamaly and president of the Catholic bishops' conference, denounces to AsiaNews: "This so-called Freedom of Religion Bill is a slur on the culture of our nation. India has long been re-
10 spected in the international community as a country of tolerance, peace and respect for cultural and religious diversity, and this is a black mark on the nation".

The law had been approved by the state
15 parliament for the first time in 2006, but the governor of the state, Pratibha Patil, had not signed it, sending it back to the chamber to be rewritten. But last week, the controversial text was approved. It prohibits conversions that
20 take place by "use of force, allurement or fraudulent means", and condemns those who practise them to five years in prison and a 50 thousand rupee [approximately € 800] fine.

The cardinal comments: "These bills,
25 which are absolutely unnecessary, are introduced by fundamentalist forces, the consequences of which are intolerance and mistrust, and loss of peaceful coexistence between peoples and communities, and eventu-
30 ally society and the nation suffer. I have always emphasised that these Freedom of Religion bills are against our constitutional freedom, our founding fathers enshrined in Article 25 of the constitution the right to the practise,
35 profession, and propagation of faith".

Besides, the anti-conversion laws are used with increasing frequency to invalidate conversions from Hinduism to Christianity. Groups of Hindu nationalists accuse the Chris-
40 tian missionaries of violating the law with the celebration of baptism, and very often attack the Christians ceremonies without waiting for a judicial inquiry. But on the other hand, the law does not provide any restrictions for those
45 who desire "to return to the true faith, Hinduism".

As Christians, concludes Cardinal Vithayathil, "This message of the resurrection cannot be restricted only to Christians, because it
50 is a message which brings hope for the world. How can we not share the Good News of Christ's victory over sin and death? We are not converting anyone with this powerful message of hope, instead we are sharing with them
55 news which is liberating".

With this ratification, six Indian states now include a law against conversions in their penal codes: Arunachal Pradesh, Gujarat, Madhya Pradesh, Chhattisgarh, Himachal Pradesh, and
60 Rajasthan. According to some Indian legal texts, the first anti-conversion law was conceived by Gandhi himself, who considered missionaries "a remnant of colonialism".

by Nirmala Carvalho
From: http://www.asianews.it/index.php?l=en&art=
11851&size=A/AsiaNews, www.asianews.it, desk@asianews.it

TASKS
---

 3 Read the article. Use a dictionary if necessary. Then get together with a partner. Explain the idea behind the new laws and assess the impact they might have.

4 Judge the function of the All Faith Committee in the novel against this backdrop.

5 Remember, Ram has often felt the importance of being a member of a specific faith.
 • Write a diary entry in which he critically reflects on his personal experiences.
 • Put the text, a sheet of paper and two coloured pens (green and blue) on your table.
 • Walk around and read at least two other texts. Give feedback on what you like about the texts (in green) and some advice on how to improve the entries (in blue).

| **KV 3.1** | **Housing in Big Indian Cities** |

© Indranil Mukherjee/AFP/Getty Images

──────── TASKS ────────

1 Name categories under which these pictures could belong.

2 Speculate on what life might be like in the different homes.

Life in the biggest slum in Mumbai

3 Let's go for a walk through Dharavi:
Watch the video about the slum and summarize the work done there.
Also explain the central idea behind the so-called redevelopment plan.

Summary: _____

_____

_____

_____

_____

Report on the government's redevelopment plan:

_____

_____

_____

_____

_____

_____

4 Together with a partner, research the current situation in Dharavi.

Life in a chawl in Mumbai

5 Together with a partner, read the text below and describe the main problems the tenants of the chawl have to face.

Life is on the Edge for Residents of Saatrasta Chawl

1 MUMBAI, AUGUST 8: "We tremble with fear every time it starts p<u>ouring</u>. The entire family moves towards the kitchen, as far away as possible from the balcony. And 5 when it rains heavily, all the families gather at one place so that we can die together when the building collapses," says 75-year-old Sitabai Sarvankar, a resident of Dayalji Velji Chawl located at Saatrasta in 10 'E' ward.

For the last four years, residents of the 95-year-old chawl have been living life on the edge. They fear <u>treading</u> on the narrow balcony which threatens to give way any 15 moment. The whole building housing 20 families can collapse any time, according to a warning by the Mumbai Building Repairs & Reconstruction Board, a division of MHADA [= Maharashtra Housing and 20 Area Development Authority). The story repeats itself in most of the 20 other buildings listed as 'dangerous' by the board this year.

The residents here are, however, refus-25 ing to move out because of a suit against their landlord and a hotel owner on the ground floor pending in the City Civil Court, the next hearing for which [is planned] for August 12. The MHADA is also a party in the case.

The Dayalji Velji Chawl is cracking on all sides and parts of the ground floor and the staircase are under water. If it does not collapse, it can get caught in a fire because of the hotel's kitchen and exposed wires inside the building.

On February 16, '95, the Repairs Board had ordered complete demolition of the building. Interestingly, however, the next year it slapped a notice on the walls of the chawl asking only the tenants of the first and second floor to move out, since the building had been identified as 'dangerous' during a pre-monsoon survey. No such notice was served to the ground floor inhabitants, [including] a hotel and a few shops.

"It is exactly this volte-face that we are opposing. We would have no problem moving out if the whole building was being demolished. In that case, we would have been sure of returning home even if it took several months to construct a new building. But the very fact that the ground floor will remain intact even though its condition is as bad as ours proves that the hotel owner and landlord have connived with MHADA," alleges Sharad Kumar Mestry, a tenant. "Look at that shop there," he points across the road. "The top floor was demolished 20 years ago and the inmates sent to transit camps. They have still not returned as no construction has taken place [so far]." […]

Residents allege that in the last four years they have been threatened by MHADA officials, police and local goons. On May 3, 97, a part of the building was set on fire, they said. "Though the fire occurred in the afternoon, all the shops and the hotel had downed their shutters before it began. Our water connection has been cut and drunks have entered the building, abused and beaten us up. When we attend court hearings, the opposite party arrives there with local goondas and mobiles. They have tried all tactics which terrorise most middle class people," residents alleged.

MHADA officials denied the allegations, saying most people are wary of living in transit camps since it becomes a problem getting an extension after six months. "MHADA does not specify a time limit for reconstruction, and living conditions in transit camps are very poor," says an official: "Fact is that transit camps are as bad as or even worse than the dilapidated buildings. People have been living there for years, sometimes with no water or electricity. That's why they continue to live in their ramshackle houses and die there instead of being treated as homeless for the rest of their lives."

From: http://www.indianexpress.com/res/web/ple/ie/daily/19990809/ige09080.html, 5 March 2008.
http://expressindia.indianexpress.com/ie/daily/19990809/ige09080.html (shortened and adapted).

Annotations
to pour: to rain heavily
to tread: to step, to walk
volte-face: reversal of opinion
to connive: work together with s.o. (negative expression)
goon: troublemaker, hired by a gang
goonda: member of a crime gang

Comparing fiction to reality

6 In the novel, all three ways of living (slums, chawls and apartment houses) are described as well.
All of them have certain advantages and/or disadvantages which are pointed out in the novel.
- Read the passages in the novel given below on your own first.
- Identify the advantages and disadvantages with a partner.
- Finally, fill in the grid and give evidence from the text.
- Be prepared to share your ideas with the rest of the class.

Example in the Novel	Advantages	Disadvantages
Living in _____ (Neelima Kumari's life: pp. 245–247, 268)		
Living in _____ (life in Ghatkopar: pp. 70–78, 81–84)		
Living in _____ (life in Dharavi: pp. 156/157)		

7 Assess if Swarup's description of the different ways of living is realistic.
Give reasons for your answer.

KV 3.2   **The Tragic Lot of the Shantarams**

1   Report on the Shantaram family's decline as described on pages 78 to 81 in *Q & A*.

2   Imagine a tragedy like the Shantarams' happened in Germany:
Explain what might have been different from India.

A Discussion on Social Security – Role Play

3   Imagine that after his "accident", Mr Shantaram finally quits alcohol. At last, the family is able to afford middle-class standard again, but he still has not forgotten how he ended up in the gutter. He believes that the only way to prevent people from experiencing the same vicious circle as he did is a social security net. At a cocktail party at a friend's house, he discusses his idea with other guests.

- Each of you will be given a role card. Prepare your position together with others who have got the same role card.
- Four pupils are chosen to discuss the matter in a small circle of chairs. Their chair is marked by a place card with the character's name at its back.
- The other pupils are the audience and build a second circle surrounding the performers.
- Members of the audience can replace a participant in the discussion that has the same role card and add their opinion.

Role Cards

Mr Shantaram
(Astronomer)

Your position:
- You have experienced how quickly everything is lost in a state without a reliable social security system, which is why you believe that India should take action to help the less fortunate.
- You admire the German system and wonder if this could also be introduced in India.

Discuss advantages and disadvantages of the different systems with your friends and give your view.

Mrs Deraiya
(Journalist)

Your position:
- You have experienced the German social security net as you wrote a series of articles about it in Germany. You are well aware of the system's advantages, but you also know about its flaws.
- You wonder if Germany will be able to keep the system running in the years to come.

Discuss advantages and disadvantages of the different systems with your friends and give your view.

Mr Singh
(Head of an Indian company)

Your position:
- You run a very successful firm and are proud of your achievements. Employees are treated with respect in your company and receive decent wages.
- You do not believe that it would be possible to keep that standard if you had to participate in a state-run social security system.

Discuss advantages and disadvantages of the different systems with your friends and give your view.

Mrs Chanda
(Government official's wife)

Your position:
- Your husband is against establishing a social security system in India because he believes that the poor would only exploit the system. In general, you have to agree with him.
- On the other hand, a former friend of yours committed suicide because she did not know how to support her family any longer.

Discuss advantages and disadvantages of the different systems with your friends and give your view.

Place Cards

Mr Shantaram
(Astronomer)

Mrs Deraiya
(Journalist)

Mr Singh
(Head of an Indian company)

Mrs Chanda
(Government official's wife)

| KV 4 | **Orphans in India** |

1 Look at the little kid and express the first thoughts that come to your mind.
Then ask yourself the following questions:
- Who should be looking after the boy?
- What dangers might he be exposed to?

 2 Let's find out about Ram's experiences in the two orphanages he is brought to.
Read again the passages given below and complete the tasks on your own.

    a After Father Timothy's death, Ram is taken to a Juvenile Home for Boys in Delhi.
Summarize the living conditions there (cf. *Q & A*, pp. 91–93, 96/97, 100/101).

_____

_____

_____

_____

     b Explain the following quote from the novel (cf. *Q & A*, pp. 92/93):

> Being sent to the Juvenile Home from Father Timothy's house was like
> a transfer from heaven to hell for me. But only when I met the other
> boys did I realize that for many of them this was their heaven.

     c In *Q & A*, Ram and Salim are taken to the "home for the crippled", which they picture as a happy
place before their arrival (cf. *Q & A*, pp. 101, 108 and 117).
- Explain how the children are made to believe that the orphanage is a fantastic place.
- Present the bitter reality under the surface.

    d After you have finished, please get together in groups of four.
- Collect the most important information about orphans in *Q & A* and place them on a poster.
- Be prepared to present your results to the class.
- Let's have a vote on the poster that best presents the main aspects of the topic.

The Orphan Crisis Exposed

1 Between "Bollywood" and American companies hiring in India, it may be hard to believe that India has an orphan crisis. India has about three times the American population living in
5 one third of the space. Introduce intense poverty, famine, drought, natural disasters, AIDS, and malaria, and you have a recipe for tragedy and, most significantly, unaccompanied children.

10 In such conditions, it is no surprise that many parents die, leaving their children to a nation unable to take care of them. On the streets, children are disturbingly vulnerable; evil adults will cripple orphaned children in
15 order to use them for begging. It is also no surprise that children are often abandoned, particularly handicapped children and baby girls (whose dowries will put unbearable financial burdens on their parents).

20 If girls are not abandoned, they might be killed soon after birth or married off at nine years old to a man 30 years older than them. I am not sure which is worse – are you?

From: © Warm Blankets Orphan Care International.
URL: http://www.indianorphans.com/, queried 03/09/2010

TASKS

---

3 Read the text and sum up the reality of orphans in India together with a partner. Particularly focus on the dangers that orphans in India are exposed to.
Use a dictionary to look up unknown words if necessary.

_____

_____

_____

_____

4 Together, find out more about the general conditions in orphan houses in India on the internet and take notes.

_____

_____

_____

_____

5 Assess whether Swarup's description of orphan houses is a realistic one.

6 Imagine Ram uses the popularity he gained from participating in *W3B* to write an open letter to a big Indian newspaper. In this letter he tells the Indian public about his own awful experiences. It is his aim to have the home closed and to free the children

- Write an article of about 200 words.
- Get together in groups of three and read your classmates' texts. Use the evaluation sheet to help each other improve the texts.
- Use your classmates' evaluation to rewrite your text again.

Evaluation Sheet: Open Letter

In groups of three, discuss and evaluate the texts you have written.
Read both your classmates' texts.
Focus on contents, structure and language.

When partner A has evaluated the text, please fold the sheet
along the dotted line so that partner B can conduct the
evaluation without being influenced by the advice given already.

	Criteria	Partner B	Partner A
Structure	Is there a logical structure (introduction, main body, conclusion)?	☐ Yes ☐ No Advice:	☐ Yes ☐ No Advice:
	Does the text contain all elements of an open letter (e. g. form of address, request for action)	☐ Yes ☐ No Advice:	☐ Yes ☐ No Advice:
Contents	Do you think the text goes along with what you have found out about orphans in the text and in your classmates' report?	☐ Yes ☐ No Advice:	☐ Yes ☐ No Advice:
	Is it in line with what you know about Ram?	☐ Yes ☐ No Advice:	☐ Yes ☐ No Advice:
	Is the text interesting? If not, how could it be improved?	☐ Yes ☐ No Advice:	☐ Yes ☐ No Advice:
Language	Did you understand everything?	☐ Yes ☐ No Advice:	☐ Yes ☐ No Advice:
	Can you spot any mistakes? (grammar or vocabulary)	☐ Yes ☐ No Advice:	☐ Yes ☐ No Advice:

| KV 5 | **The Wonderful World of Bollywood** |

1 Tell me about your favourite Hollywood star.

2 Look at the film poster below. The actors you can see are just as popular in India as your favourite stars are in Europe and North America.
Describe and interpret the poster (the German title might help you).

Watching a Bollywood film scene

 3 We are going to watch a scene from *Paheli*. While watching, think about why such a film is so popular in India.

Placemat activity: The real and the fictitious world of Bollywood

 4 Get together in groups of four.

  • Sit opposite each other and put the placemat worksheet in the middle. You are responsible for the tasks written on the square (**A** to **D**) that is in front of you.
  • Read the text or excerpts from the novel your tasks refers to. Look up unknown words in a dictionary.
  • Write the answers to your tasks onto your part of the placemat or use a spare sheet of paper.
  • The blank space in the middle (**E**) is the area all of you can contribute to as soon as you have finished your respective tasks. Share your knowledge with the other members of your group and sum up the most important aspects in the middle of the placemat.
  • Be prepared to present the results of your placemat activity to class.

Placemat

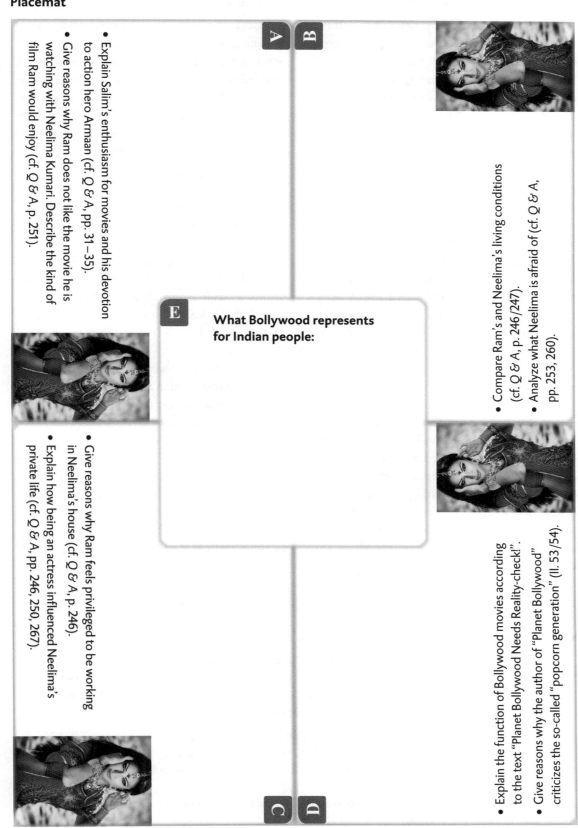

A

- Explain Salim's enthusiasm for movies and his devotion to action hero Armaan (cf. *Q & A*, pp. 31–35).
- Give reasons why Ram does not like the movie he is watching with Neelima Kumari. Describe the kind of film Ram would enjoy (cf. *Q & A*, p. 251).

B

- Compare Ram's and Neelima's living conditions (cf. *Q & A*, p. 246/247).
- Analyze what Neelima is afraid of (cf. *Q & A*, pp. 253, 260).

E

What Bollywood represents for Indian people:

C

- Give reasons why Ram feels privileged to be working in Neelima's house (cf. *Q & A*, p. 246).
- Explain how being an actress influenced Neelima's private life (cf. *Q & A*, pp. 246, 250, 267).

D

- Explain the function of Bollywood movies according to the text "Planet Bollywood Needs Reality-check!".
- Give reasons why the author of "Planet Bollywood" criticizes the so-called "popcorn generation" (ll. 53/54).

Text for Group Member D: Planet Bollywood Needs Reality-check!

1 [...] I would like to thank the saint, Valmiki for opening my eyes to the reality of the great Indian lack of sensibility. For it was Valmiki Jayanti that pulled me out of bed on a lazy
5 morning to watch an 11 am show of Shyam Benegal's *Welcome To Sajjanpur*. Welcomed by the arid grin of the torch guy I sluggishly walked into a practically empty auditorium. A few minutes trickled in some sleazy lovebirds
10 who wished to employ the darkness for their exotic pursuits.

Anyways, coming to what really shocked me after the screening of two and a half hours of pure cinematic genius was the realisation
15 that I belonged to a generation that gyrated on mind numbing music and was happily feeding on movies which were called "slice of life" but had practically no story lines except the rising hemlines.

20 Stating it simply, Bollywood is a money minting entertainment and service industry that caters to a wide variety of audience by playing to their social and emotional needs. There is no sure shot formula of success at the
25 box office, is what I have often heard them say but most blockbusters are a usual combination of glamour, action and melodrama. But what is upsetting is a complete exhaustion of an intelligent audience which I thought would
30 be appreciative of an honest and scathing social satire like the Benegal's movie.

With over 300 movies being released in a year, one cannot even imagine the girth of economics in this industry. The interesting part is
35 on one hand we have actors who even when graying try and adorn themselves with lover boy roles and serenade their size zero heroines in romantic pursuits. While characters like Mahadev and Munni Bai of Sajjanpur are
40 left to rot in empty auditoriums as they try to tell the people of this country about the ground reality and how the grass root level problems can be solved. But very nonchalantly many of us believe in closing our eyes lit-
45 erally and metaphorically dance to "bhutani de".

Planet Bollywood needs a reality check. Any form of art is responsible for generating beauty as well as meaning. Beauties galore for
50 sure, but ironically there is a complete lack of meaning or value as far as most movies are concerned.

The surprising element is, that this popcorn generation which I thought will be shoul-
55 dering complex issues that the future will unleash somehow finds meaning and entertainment in bare chested men with rippling muscles and coloured hair extensions rather than realising that a part of their country's popu-
60 lation is battling problems of poverty, illiteracy and mafia politics.

For most a next Friday release is lined up so who cares if Benegal is telling the harsh truth?

From: http://www.merinews.com

After the placemat activity

5 Let's analyze the attitude Swarup expresses by letting Bollywood actress Neelima Kumari commit suicide. Each of you will be asked contribute his or her thoughts, but wait until the person next to you has finished, before you start talking. Do not comment on statements you consider wrong, only focus on putting your opinion across and giving reasons for it.

6 Imagine that Neelima wanted the world to know why she committed suicide.
   • Think of a suicide note that she might have left. Write about 200 words.
   • Get together in groups of four. Read your classmates' texts on your own first.
   • Then decide on the best text in your group.
   • Together, improve this text as far as contents, structure and language are concerned.
   • Read out your text in class.

| **KV 6.1** | **Women in India – No Chance from the very Start of their Lives?** |

1 Look at the question on the board: "What are your plans for the future?"
  - All female pupils answer the question without talking. They take a piece of chalk each and write their answer down. If there is a reaction to the answer, reply in written form as well.
  - The male pupils can comment in written form on the girls' ideas, or ask further questions.

2 Assess whether an Indian girl has the same expectations and dreams as you.

3 Read again pages 299 to 302 and 304 to 306 in the novel Q & A.
  - Briefly summarize prostitute Nita's background and her family's "tradition".
  - Outline and explain Nita's situation by the time she meets Ram.

Being a Girl in India – A Vicious Circle

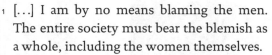

Text 1

1 [...] I am by no means blaming the men. The entire society must bear the blemish as a whole, including the women themselves.

[The percentage of female literacy] is still 5 a good 20 percentage points less than that of their male counterpart[s]. The disparity is even higher in rural areas where over 63 % [...] women remain unlettered.

[One main reason for low school-] en-10 rolment [of girls] is that families find it more beneficial to entrust young or adolescent girls with household duties than send them to school. This is also the reason for high drop-out rates besides early marriages. A 15 good education not only becomes a gateway to a woman's economic independence but [...] helps her achieve better health, hygiene and be a support to her family.

While there have been several courts 20 [...] guaranteeing the right of earning the same pay for the same amount of work, it remains a distant reality in practice. This is particularly true of the unorganized sector especially dealing with manual labour 25 where the Minimum Wage Act norms are often violated. [...] Unequal pay for the same job happens to be one problem that men sometimes have to face as well. [...]

by Akrita Reyar;
from: http://www.zeenews.com/zeeexclusive/2009-03-31/
474684news.html (shortened and adapted).
by courtesy of www.zeenews.com, © Zee News Limited

Text 2

1 Women are highly discriminated against when applying for a job. Men are preferred in many positions so that women are sometimes forced to stay at home or take over 5 bad and poorly paid jobs. The unequal job situation leads to severe poverty among women.

In order to break through the circle of poverty, families consider marriage at an 10 early age an adequate solution. Many young girls are getting married and become very young mothers. As the use of contraceptives is still a taboo in many regions, families often have six or more children. Feeding 15 such a big family can lead into poverty again. And as education is an expensive sector in India, children – and especially girls – from rather poor families are not likely to get access to schools.

© Judith C. Säckl, 2010

— **TASK** —

4 Read the two texts above. Together with a partner, fill in the steps of the vicious circle Indian girls often experience (the text and the novel might help you).
Then get together with another team and compare your results.

Picturing the Vicious Circle

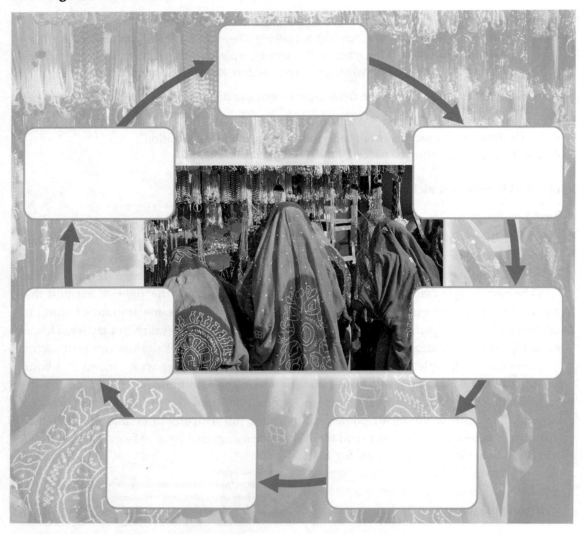

5 Compare the general situation of women in India (as shown in the vicious circle) to the lot of Nita
and Gudiya Shantaram in *Q & A*.

_____

_____

_____

_____

_____

_____

_____

6 Assess whether this vicious circle can be broken.

KV 6.2 | Aid Organisations for Women in India

1 Together with a partner, use the Internet to find out more about an organization that wants to improve women's living conditions in India.

- Prepare a presentation in which you introduce the organization. You can either prepare a poster or a PowerPoint presentation. Your presentation should not be longer than five to eight minutes.
- The following information should be included in your presentation:
  - Name of the organization
  - Web address
  - Basic information about the organization (e.g. date of foundation, aims, target groups)
  - Activities/Projects
  - Achievements so far

- While the other groups are presenting, use the grid below to evaluate their presentations. Be prepared to give them feedback if asked for it.

Evaluation grid

	Criteria	Information given / Comment on quality of presentation	☺	😐	☹
Group	Name of organisation presented				
Contents	Principles employed by organisation				
	Strategies used by organisation to achieve goals				
Quality of Presentation	Logic of structure				
	Means of visualization				
	Use of language, audibility				
	Contact with audience (dealing with questions, body language, eye contact)				

2 Look at your notes again. Assess whether there are certain principles or strategies employed by all the different organisations.

Creative Writing

3 Choose one of the following two tasks:

a Ram is looking for help in order to free Nita and turns to an international aid organisation. Imagine you are an acquaintance of his. Because your business English is far better than his, Ram asks you to write an e-mail to the organisation for him.

- Choose one of the aid organisations you have heard about today. Your choice should be based on which organisation is suited best for the cause of freeing Nita.
- Present the case to the organisation, ask for help and suggest activities to help Nita get free.
- Don't forget to consider the tight network of oppression she is caught in.

Write about 200 words.

b Work with a partner and write a dialogue between Nita and a friend of hers whom she encounters after Ram has freed her.

- Include Nita's thoughts and feelings about Ram as well as her and her friend's opinion on education, independence, chances they have (had) in life, their families, traditions and love.
- Be prepared to perform the dialogue in front of class.

4 Explain why it is so important to Nita to have a surname (cf. *Q & A*, pp. 299, 360).

KV 7	**Arranged Marriages**

The Tribune Matrimonials

Suitable match for Punjabi (upper caste) Hindu bachelor lawyer, flourishing practice, Chandigarh, 43/6', handsome personality, only son of retired Class-I Officer. One married sister, well-connected family with liberal religious views. No bars. Contact 98141-95888. princecharming@gmail.com C4-289

Wanted: professional match preferably M.Pharm./B.Pharm. for Chandigarh born Brahmin boy 31. 3. 1983, 3:37 pm, 5'–5", B. Pharm. from India postgraduate from Britain, having permanent Pharmacist job in Britain, Himachal origin, British national.
Mail to: 10036M@box.tribuneindia.com C4-147132

From: http://www.tribuneindia.com/2010/20100207/class-m.htm

Annotations
Chandigarh: town in India; **43/6':** 43 years old, 6 feet tall (about 180 cm); **no bars:** no restrictions
M. Pharm./B. Pharm: Master in Pharmacy or Bachelor in Pharmacy (university degrees)
Brahmin boy: member of supreme caste
5'–5": required body height between 5 feet and 5 feet 5 inches (between 152 cm and 165 cm)

TASKS

1 Read these marriage advertisements (Indian English: "matrimonials") from the personal column of an Indian newspaper. Explain what they can tell you about Indian society.

2 Imagine there is a line drawn from one side of the classroom to the other. As indicated by the two sheets of paper that have been put up, standing close to one end means "in favour of arranged marriages". Standing close to the other end means "against arranged marriages".
  • Make up your mind about what you think about this way of getting to know your spouse and position yourself along the line to make your opinion known.
  • Be prepared to justify your choice.

Positionslinie

in favour of arranged marriages

against arranged marriages

Expertenpuzzle

3 The concept of arranged marriages is still very common in India. Let's take a closer look at it. We need to split up the class in two groups:

Group A reads the article "Arranged Marriages – Facts" and summarizes the positive aspects as presented. Use a dictionary to look up unknown words if necessary.

Group B finds out how the issue is presented in the novel (cf. Q & A, pp. 292–294, 309/310, 313–315). In particular, concentrate on Ram's friend Lajwanti's expectations, the difficulties she has to face and how she is going to solve them.

- Firstly, work on your respective subjects with a partner and write down the answer to your task.
- Then get together with two pupils from the other group and present your results to each other.

Group A: Arranged Marriages – Facts

1 **Love is in the air …**
To westerners who put a lot of emphasis on love and marriage or shall we say – love before marriage – love is the only thing
5 you need to be happy. But for societies who believe that arranged marriages will flourish and endure forever, love, at least for the time being, can take the back seat.

Arranged Marriages: Fact # 1
10 Arranged marriages are viewed as a social and economic necessity, the terms of which are agreed upon by the families of the future groom and bride. The question of whether the bride and groom are in love
15 is not a priority; what's important is that the marriage is stable with staying power.

Point of clarification: indeed, love makes the world go round. We all want to be madly and passionately in love. But
20 just because arranged marriages are not premised exclusively on love, it doesn't mean that it does not exist in the relationship. It may be born on day 1 of the marriage or can grow after a few years. We
25 should not be misled [to believe] that spouses in arranged marriages have no say about their partners. In some countries the man or woman can refuse a selected spouse. Because consent by both is im-
30 perative, who is to say that love does not or cannot exist? […]

© www.professorshouse.com

Arranged Marriages: Fact # 2

35 [...] It is a fact that despite the few and isolated stories covered by the media of young women being forced into marriages, there are equally, if not more, successful arranged marriages. The argument 40 is that because parents know their children best and have the wisdom and wherewithal to select the best candidate, the marriage will benefit from the support and encouragement of their elders and 45 hence will be durable and permanent. There are significantly fewer divorces or separations between people of arranged marriages.

Point of clarification: we need to be 50 careful about taking arranged marriages from the perspective of the divorce rate. It is true that only a few arranged marriages end in divorce, but is the reason really the arranged marriage itself or the fact that in 55 more traditional and conservative societies, people usually don't get divorced anyway and stay within the marriage hoping to work things out?

From: © www.professorshouse.com

4 In your group, judge Swarup's picture of arranged marriages as presented in the novel.

_____

_____

_____

_____

Talk show

5 Now we are going to have a talk show.

- Take a card which describes the character you will play in the show.

- Look for classmates who have the same role as you do. Together, prepare suitable arguments to support your character's view. Use your background knowledge on arranged marriages.

- Be prepared to perform your part in the role play in front of class. During the play, the audience can ask the participants questions in the talk show.

Samir Bhatnagar

Character details:
You are a young Indian man living in the UK. Your parents want you to marry an Indian girl and have already started to arrange the marriage with a suitable candidate from Mumbai.

Problem:
You are in love with an Indian girl you have met in London and would like to marry her.

Aim:
Convince your parents that they should leave this decision to you.

Rajani Charan

Character details:
You are an Indian girl who lives in the UK. Your parents are liberal-minded and allow you to see your boyfriend Samir. They like him a lot.

Problem:
You hear that Samir's parents have already started to arrange a marriage for him with a girl from Mumbai. You are scared of losing him.

Aim:
Convince Samir's parents that the concept of arranged marriages is completely outdated.

Mr Bhatnagar

Character details:
You are a middle-aged man living in India. You have already started to arrange a marriage for your son Samir with an Indian girl from Mumbai.

Problem:
Your son tells you he is in love with an Indian girl he met in London where he currently lives. You are furious because it is very disrespectful to reject the bride the parents have chosen.

Aim:
Convince your son that you know what is good for him.

Mrs Bhatnagar

Character details:
You are a middle-aged woman living in India. You have already started to arrange a marriage for your son Samir with an Indian girl from Mumbai.

Problem:
Your son tells you he is in love with an Indian girl he met in London where he currently lives. You cannot understand your son. Your husband was chosen by your parents and you have been quite happily married for 25 years now.

Aim:
Convince your son that you know what is good for him.

Steve King

Character details:
You are a young British man. Your best friend Samir Bhatnagar and his Indian girlfriend Rajani Charan are desperate because his parents are planning an arranged marriage for him.

Problem:
Personally, you are against the concept of arranged marriages. But you are a sensitive person and like to consider both sides of an issue before making a decision.

Aim:
You calmly try to explain the meaning of true love to Samir's parents.

Presenter

Character details:
You are the host of a talk show. Read the other role cards to get to know your guests.

Aim:
- Try to make the guests express their points of view in an understandable and detailed way.
- Focus on conversation rules and make sure that every guest gets the chance to speak.
- Once in a while, sum up the guests' points of view and ask selected guests for some further contributions.
- Think of questions you could ask both the guests and the audience.

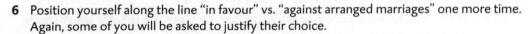

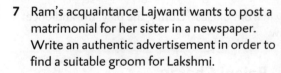

6 Position yourself along the line "in favour" vs. "against arranged marriages" one more time. Again, some of you will be asked to justify their choice.

7 Ram's acquaintance Lajwanti wants to post a matrimonial for her sister in a newspaper. Write an authentic advertisement in order to find a suitable groom for Lakshmi.

| KV 8 | **Tourism and Travelling in India** |

Ram's Journey through India

1 Watch the scene from the movie *Slumdog Millionaire* without the original audio. Instead, you will hear typical Indian music. Point out what makes Indian public transport differ from the German way of travelling.

2 Get together in groups, choose one of the following tasks and present your results in class later on.

  a Analyse how tourism is presented in the novel.
  - Name the place(s) where Ram meets tourists and explain what the tourists like about it/them. (cf. *Q & A*, pp. 277–282, 294–297)
  - Analyse how the tourists are portrayed in the novel.
  - Examine how Ram feels about the tourists.

  b Examine Ram's journeys through India.
  - Read again about Ram's journeys (cf. *Q & A*, pp. 84–86, 91, 103/104, 155/156, 173/174, 190/191) and take notes on the respective points of departure and arrival as well as on the reasons for these journeys.
  - Then draw his route on the map. Use symbols/colours to show the different stages of Ram's journey and arrows to indicate the direction he is travelling in.

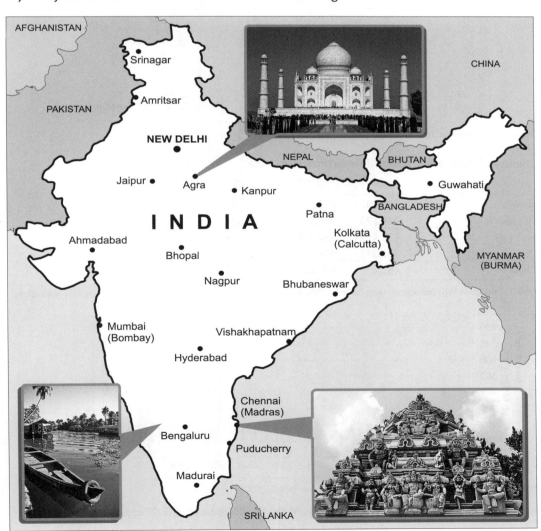

Tourism and Travelling in India – Background information

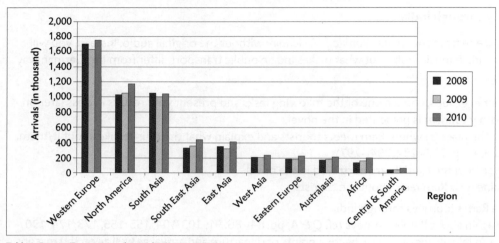

Table 1: Foreign Tourist Arrivals in India (2008–2010)

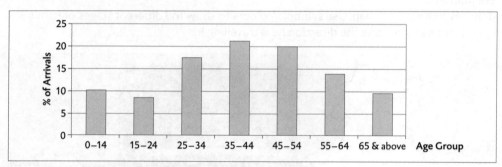

Table 2: Age-Group-wise classification of Foreign Tourist Arrivals in India, 2010

Country of Destination	National Departures from India		
	2007	2008	2009
Kuwait	653,392	673,671	733,117
Singapore	748,728	778,303	725,624
Malaysia	422,452	550,738	589,838
USA	567,045	598,971	549,474
China	462,450	436,625	448,942

Table 3: Destination-Wise Number of Indian Nationals Departures from India (2007–2009), showing the top five holiday destinations.

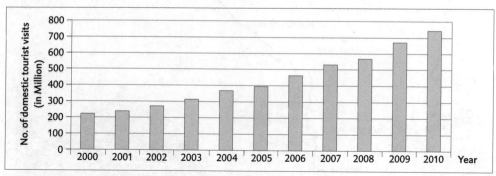

Table 4: Annual Domestic Tourists Visits to the (Indian) States (2000–2010)

From: http://tourism.gov.in/writereaddata/CMSPagePicture/file/Primary%20Content/MR/pub-OR-statistics/2010Statistics.pdf

3 Analyse the statistics and outline how domestic and foreign tourism developed from 2008 to 2010 as far as Indian holiday destinations are concerned.

4 Give reasons why India seems especially popular with certain tourist age groups.

5 Speculate on possible reasons for Indian foreign and domestic holiday destinations.

6 Now have a closer look at Swarup's picture of tourists in India:
- Judge what message Swarup wanted to convey by portraying tourists in India the way he did. Make notes of your ideas and sort them before sharing them with the class.

REALITY CHECK!

_____

_____

_____

_____

- Let's discuss your ideas in the form of a round robin. Everybody is allowed to say only one sentence. Try not to repeat aspects that have already been mentioned and do not comment on other people's statements.

7 Imagine you could get hold on a ticket to India and could stay there for a few weeks.
- Collect advantages and disadvantages on your own first.

Advantages	Disadvantages

- Then explain if you would seize the opportunity or leave it. Give reasons for your decision.

| KV 9.1 | Q & A on Screen – *Slumdog Millionaire* |

1 Imagine you had a great idea for a sensational plot:
- Decide whether you would prefer to write a screenplay or a novel.
- Justify your decision by pointing out the advantages and disadvantages of both film and novel concerning their prospects of conveying a plot. Fill in the grid.

	Novel	Movie
Means of conveying a plot		
Advantages		
Disadvantages		

2 We are going to watch a scene from *Slumdog Millionaire*.
- As preparation, skim pages 108 and 116 to 119 of *Q & A* again.
- Then watch the scene. Use the grid below to make notes on what has been changed in the movie adaption in comparison to the novel.

Novel	Movie

3 Analyse the effects of the modification of the plot.

Evaluating film and novel

Mixed Reactions to *Slumdog Millionaire*'s Victory

1 … And the Oscar goes to (drumroll, please) … *Slumdog Millionaire*!! The unexpected box-office hit took home one of the biggest awards of last night, Best Picture.

5 In the film, a young boy living in the poorest area of Mumbai, India, ends up winning on India's "Who Wants to Be a Millionaire" show. Though the film's storyline was, admittedly, a little fantastical, it accurately depicts 10 the lives of the many impoverished people living in India.

Seeing this type of poverty for the first time is a shock to our Western eyes. Unlike the U.S., in many developing countries, there are no 15 government-subsidized programs like our welfare system for impoverished people. Many third world countries cannot afford basic infrastructure that we take for granted – like street lights and roads – let alone establish 20 soup kitchens or a federal food stamp program.

And *Slumdog*'s story of hope and triumph set against the gritty backdrop of Mumbai's slums and corrupt police force won the hearts of Americans and the Academy alike.

25 However, not all are happy with the movie. Yesterday, *The New York Times* posted a piece describing the protests that have occurred in India against the movie. Protesters object to the word "slumdog" [as they do not want to 30 be compared to dogs. An Indian activist] claims that referring to people in the slums as dogs has violated their human rights. He even filed a lawsuit demanding that the title of the movie be changed."

35 Director Danny Boyle reacted to the criticism and protests, saying "I was expecting a full-on response because it's a very passionate place. I know some people don't like the film for very complicated reasons, and some peo- 40 ple adore it for very simple reasons."

So, what do you think? Is the movie good for spreading awareness of poverty in India and elsewhere? Or is it a violation of the Universal Declaration of Human Rights? […]

Shamsa Mangalji: Mixed Reactions to Slumdog Millionaire's Victory.
URL: http://www.dosomething.org/blog/celebsgonegood/mixed-reactions-slumdog-millionaire

─────── **TASKS** ───────

4 Read the blog entry and look up unknown words in a dictionary if necessary.
Get together with a partner and outline people's reactions to the film.

5 Together, think of other reasons that could have caused some people's hostile view towards the film.

6 Judge whether or not *Slumdog Millionaire* is a "violation of the Universal Declaration of Human Rights" (ll. 43/44).

7 Write a review of *Q & A* in which you express what you liked/did not like about the novel and whether you consider it a suitable means for dealing with the topic of "India".

KV 9.2 | India – A Jigsaw Puzzle

You have got to know the different sides of India while working with the novel *Q & A*.
Below, you see ten pieces of a puzzle. Write the ten most interesting aspects that come to your mind in connection with India on those puzzle pieces, cut them out and then rebuild a puzzle of the country of India.

| **KV 10** | **Klausurvorschlag mit Erwartungshorizont** |

"Slumdog" in Mumbai: "My eyes couldn't believe it."
by Andrew Buncombe

1 They awoke before dawn, determined not to miss out on the excitement unfolding thousands of miles away. And when – in scenes which echo those in the film – the good news
5 turned to more good news and then even better news, they danced and sang and cheered.

In the teeming neighbourhoods of Mumbai where *Slumdog Millionaire* is set, crowds of children and adults gathered around televi-
10 sion sets to cheer for the local stars who had made the transformation from the narrow, filthy alleyways to the silver screen.

Azharuddin Mohammed Ismail, 10, and nine-year-old Rubiana Ali, both from a slum
15 in the Bandra district on the outskirts of Mumbai, were flown to Los Angeles for the ceremony. Azhar lives in a shack of plastic tarpaulins and mouldy blankets, while Rubiana shares a tin-roofed lean-to with her parents and her six
20 brothers and sisters.

But yesterday they were stars, masters of a different universe. "My eyes couldn't believe that I was seeing Rubiana in America," said Saba Qureshi, Rubiana's best friend, who
25 watched the action on one of the few local televisions. Sohail Qureshi, Saba's father and Rubiana's neighbour, added: "It seems like happiness is falling from the sky."

The movie's success was celebrated with
30 fervor in India, with the Prime Minister, Manmohan Singh, offering his congratulations and saying that "the winners have done India proud".

Initially, however, the movie's focus on
35 India's widespread grinding poverty and the fact that its director is a foreigner stirred considerable controversy. It would not be good for India's image, argued many commentators.

Some social activists organized demonstra-
40 tions to protest against the residents of poor neighbourhoods being referred to as "slumdogs".[1]

Perhaps surprisingly, among the movie's warmest fans have been those people who live
45 in the poorest, broken neighbourhoods of India's swarming cities and who can testify to the realism of the poverty portrayed.

Yesterday, in a run-down Delhi neighbourhood known as Coolie's Camp – comprising
50 about 350 tiny homes squeezed in next to one of the city's more expensive areas – residents learnt of the film's success and were pleased it had secured international success. Many had watched it, either on DVD or at a local cinema.

55 "It's a film that shows the reality. It's different from other films," said 25-year-old Ajay Singh. "The things in the film are real and other movies do not show this. I'm very happy this film has got recognition."

60 Deepak, 22, who gave just one name, said: "It's a film worth watching for its reality. Other films are from a different world, a different Delhi, a different India."

Yet no one believed the movie's success or
65 its focus on India's poverty would change their own situation. "This film will become an icon, but the grass roots issues will be lost," said Yaswant Singh, a hotel worker. "Even if the politicians come here, even if the NGOs come
70 here, they just come for a short time and then they go away."

From: http://www.independent.co.uk/news/world/asia/slumdog-in-mumbai-8216my-eyes-couldn8217t-believe-it8217-1630310.html © Andrew Buncombe, The Independent, February 24, 2009.

1 In addition to that, they accuse the movie of conveying a one-sided image of India that stresses the negative sides and focuses too much on picturing the violation of human rights and the most awful living conditions to be found in India.

Comprehension/Analysis

1 The article mentions that the film *Slumdog Millionaire* has "stirred considerable controversy" (ll. 36/37). Use the information given in the article as well as your background knowledge to explain what attitudes exist towards the film. Write about 150 words. (10 credits)

2 Compare *Slumdog Millionaire* to Bollywood movies.
Use your background knowledge and refer to the novel *Q & A*.
Write between 150 and 200 words. (20 credits)

Comment

3 Politicians are thinking about demolishing India's biggest slum, "Dharavi", and realizing a governmental redevelopment plan.
Decide whether Dharavi should be preserved or demolished. Use your background knowledge to give reasons for your opinion.
- Present either two pros **or** two cons in your comment.
- Write about 200 to 250 words. (40 credits)

(total: 70 credits)

Lösungsvorschläge

| KV 1 | **Many Stories to Tell**

First impressions on Q & A / Slumdog Millionaire

1 Possible ideas:
- **What you liked most about the novel:** interesting characters, catchy plot
- **Things you did not understand:** strange traditions for non-Indian readers, confusing structure of the novel, stories seem unconnected
- **Aspects that interested you most:** Is this a realistic portrayal of India?

Stories within a Story – The Structure of Q & A and Slumdog Millionaire

2 a Following the chronological order of the events, both situations happen at the end. Ram (in the film he is called Jamal K. Malik) ends up as a contestant for "Who wants to be a millionaire" (called "Who wants to earn a billion?" in the novel) in order to win money to free his girlfriend Nita. After winning the quiz show, he is arrested, accused of fraud and questioned by the police.
All the stories told in the various chapters chronologically occur before the quiz show and the questioning as Ram tells them while talking to his lawyer.

b In the novel and in the movie, the scene is presented at the very beginning.

3

Chronological order	Plot/Setting in Q & A	Chapter (Number)
2	Juvenile home in Delhi: Ram meets Salim	A Thought for the Crippled (4)
7	• Life in Dharavi, job at Jimmy's restaurant: story about Voodoo • Bumps into Salim: story called "licence to kill"	Hold On To Your Buttons (6) Licence to Kill (9)
6	Job as a tourist guide in Agra	X Gkrz Opknu/The Thirteenth Question (11/12)
3	Mumbai, home for the crippled	A Thought for the Crippled (4)
8	Quiz show, questioning, conversation with lawyer	Prologue, The Thirteenth Question (12), linking part between stories
1	St Mary's orphanage, adoption by Father Timothy	The Burden of a Priest (2)
4	Job at Neelima Kumari's house	Tragedy Queen (10)
5	Ram's way to Agra: story about murder on the Western express	Murder on the Western Express (7)

4 The novel does not follow the chronological order of events. The order in the novel follows the chronology of questions which Ram can only answer because of the experiences connected to the specific events and sites. It is the questions that decide the order of the stories told.

5 These elements form the beginning and the end of the novel. They appear several times throughout the novel, at the beginning of many of the chapters. They connect the stories and are the outer framework, while the single episodes taken from Ram's life function as internal action.

Mögliches Tafelbild:

Stories within a Story – The Structure of Q & A
• elements of quiz show, questioning and conversation with lawyer: framework   • episodes taken from Ram's life: internal action   • stories told in Q & A grouped according to order of the questions

6 Swarup is particularly interested in theories regarding memory. He has always wondered what is going on in the mind of a quiz show contestant. This is why he decided to let Ram tell the stories from his memory instead of simply experiencing them. In addition to that, the author likes the tension created by the two strands of the novel. He took it as a challenge to weave a net out of the story creating the framework and the internal action with the intention of creating a story that could be understood and followed by the reader. Besides, he needed the questions as a kind of backbone to credibly lead to the stories told by Ram.

KV 2   One Country – Many Religions

1 Individual solutions

2 a The All Faith Committee visits Father Timothy and wants to make sure that the orphan is given a religiously correct name. As the boy's faith is not known, they agree on the name "Ram Mohammad Thomas" in order to satisfy all three possible religions (Hinduism, Islam, Christianity). In addition, he might have been given a fourth name, but the Sikh member of the committee is absent that day.

b The different religions seem not to mix and live separately. Religion is also used as an excuse for murder (e.g. the attack on Salim's family in the village). People are judged and get jobs only because they believe in the "right" god.

c His attitude is somewhat pragmatic. He is interested in every religion and likes them all. For him, the differences are not important.

d He carefully chooses his name according to the situation in a very clever way. His different names are of advantage to him as he can choose the most helpful one. He might be seen as opportunistic as he always picks the most suitable: by doing so, he gets his job as Bollywood actress Neelima Kumari's servant, whereas Salim fails because of his Muslim name.

"Black" Day for India: New Anti-Conversion Law in Rajasthan

3 The anti-conversion laws are supposed to ensure freedom of religion. However, in reality they have been introduced by religious fundamentalists whose aim it is to strengthen Hinduism by force. This becomes clear as the anti-conversion laws are used more often to prevent conversions from Hinduism to Christianity (and not the other way round).

Mögliches Tafelbild:

One Country – Many Religions
Reality in Rajasthan: • Anti-conversion laws (2008) • Background: promotion of equality of religions • Reality: forceful means of support for the Hindu faith in northern India

4 Tensions between the religions are not stressed in the novel. Swarup presents a conciliatory point of view towards the coexistence of the different faiths in form of the All Faith Committee: It is there to ensure that all religions are granted a say in matters that concern more than one of the different congregations.

5 *Sample solution:*
Dear diary,
Who on earth has the right to judge people only on their religious beliefs? People kill each other for not believing in the same god; people are badly discriminated against only because they pray in the "wrong" temple, or mosque, or church, whatever is called their holy place.
Salim's family was burnt to death by so-called religious people who don't even know about the concept of mercy and love, which is part of every religion!
Unfortunately, I won't be able to put an end to all the crying and dying over religion in India, but at least I have found out how to survive, myself! I know how to handle the tensions now! Lucky me, I have three names and can switch my religious affiliation according to the situation, isn't that great?

| **KV 3.1** | **Housing in Big Indian Cities** |

1 slums (pictures A and B), chawls (C and D), luxury houses/apartments (E and F)

2 Possible solutions:
- **slums/Dharavi** (India's biggest slum in Mumbai):
  In the pictures at the top (A and B), there are ramshackle huts that seem to be old and dirty. There is probably an awful smell in the air as there is rubbish everywhere. People living there must be very poor, and the living conditions must be hard.

- **chawls** (a type of housing often found in Mumbai, about four or five floors, people usually have one or two rooms and have to share the toilets):
  In the pictures in the middle (C and D), the houses look quite shabby; people's clothes are hanging outside. There is probably no privacy in such an apartment house as you live very close to your neighbours. People living here must be quite poor, but better off than those living in the slums.

- **luxury apartment houses:**
  The houses in pictures E and F look quite modern and clean. These photos could also have been taken in a big city in the USA or in Europe. If this is India, the apartments are probably very expensive so that only upper-class people can afford them. Life in such a house is likely to be very comfortable. In contrast to pictures B or C, hardly any people can be seen.

Life in the biggest slum in Mumbai

3 Summary: In Mumbai's largest slum, more than one million people live in brick and tin shanties on 550 acres. They mainly live from pottery, leather tanning and recycling plastics. Now investors plan to rebuild the area and the government approves of the idea.

Report on the government's redevelopment plan: The plan is to relocate people into small flats in big buildings and let them start a new life. Basic standards of living would be ensured thanks to sewage, running water and sanitation. However, without the jobs in the pottery industry and their network in Dharavi, they wouldn't have any basis to live from. Pottery and leather works will be banned from the area as they cause too much pollution. In general, people want to be granted a much bigger say in the whole affair.

4 At the moment, the redevelopment activities have been halted due to the protests of grassroot organisations. This opposition is formed by NGOs, e.g. the Society for the Promotion of Area Resource Centres (SPARC), the National Slum Dwellers Federation (NSDF) and women's savings groups such as Mahila Milan. Those organisations as well as an expert group appointed by the government demand that the redevelopment process should focus much more on the situation of the slum dwellers and the question on how to relocate them appropriately.

Life in a chawl in Mumbai

5 Tenants have to live in run-down houses that might even endanger their lives. They have to deal with bad living conditions (no water, no electricity). The inhabitants are against the demolition plans as it seems clear that these plans only follow the aim of getting rid of the tenants so that the houses can be used for a more profitable purpose. They have to oppose the landlord's threats and the violence he uses to make them move out.

Comparing fiction to reality

6 Example in the Novel	Advantages	Disadvantages
Living in **a nice flat** (Neelima Kumari's life: pp. 245–247, p. 268)	• comfortable lifestyle • perfect living conditions • life in luxury without fear for one's existence **Novel:** "Neelima Kumari's flat ... carpets and paintings." (p. 246)	• anonymity • no social environment **Novel:** "They discover her body ... the smell." (p. 268)
Living in **a chawl** (life in Ghatkopar: pp. 70–78, 81–84)	• neighbours help each other (opposition against landlord) • social network **Novel:** "What happened to Neelima ... a common roof" (p. 70); "I jump down ... grasp my hand." (p. 82)	• poverty • run down apartments • crowded houses • dependence on landlord **Novel:** "A bundle ... in slums like Dharavi." (p. 70)

Living in **a slum** (life in Dharavi: pp. 156/157)	• solidarity • social and economic network **Novel:** "But I am not alone …" (p. 156); "They work in … illegal shops" (p. 157)	• awful living conditions: dirt • poor sanitation • no privacy • diseases and death as part of everyday life **Novel:** "I live in a corner … and no sanitation." (p. 156)

7 Swarup pictures housing in big Indian cities in a realistic way. Thus, the reader gains an insight into real Indian life. For example, the inhabitants of the Saatrasta chawl described in the newspaper article live in a building that is very much like the one, where Ram, Salim and the Shantarams live (cf. pp. 84/85: there is a broken railing which has not been fixed by the landlord yet and poor living conditions).

KV 3.2   The Tragic Lot of the Shantarams

1 The Shantaram family's decline started when an envious colleague takes credit for Mr Shantaram's discovery of a new star. Turning into a bitter person, Mr Shantaram started drinking, lost his job and couldn't pay for the family's home any more. His wife had to helplessly watch the situation get worse and worse. Since Mr Shantaram could only get temporary and badly paid jobs, the family had to move to a cheap chawl. It is very unlikely that they will be able to rise again socially.

2 Possible aspects:
- Germany as welfare state: financial support for the family
- intervention by hospital and the government office of youth welfare likely after Gudiya's accident
- bearable living conditions provided by social security system
- possibility of Gudiya and her mother finding shelter at a women's refuge

A Discussion on Social Security – Role Play

3 Possible arguments:
- **Mr Shantaram (Astronomer):**
  - Every citizen has got the right to live under conditions that preserve his or her dignity.
  - As in Germany, basic accommodation and health care should be provided by the state.
  - The state should not abandon citizens to their fate.
  - Poor Indian children do not have any chance to lead a better life than their parents in the future.
- **Mrs Deraiya (Journalist):**
  - In Germany, being poor is not life-threatening.
  - The dignity of citizens is preserved through the state's help.
  - Poor people's children still have chances because their families are supported financially.

– With more and more old people, who do not work anymore and therefore contribute nothing to the social system, it is questionable if the German state can continue to provide the poor with financial support. There has already been a reform: due to the Agenda 2010, people receive less benefits if they do not take jobs that have been offered to them, or if they remain unemployed for more than one year.

- **Mr Singh (Head of an Indian company):**
  - A social welfare system might prevent people from working for low wages.
  - This would endanger the Indian economy because companies would have to save money they contribute to the system. Labour costs would be cut.
  - In India, we believe people are responsible for their fortune and not the state.
  - It would be hard-working people who have to pay to support the poor.

- **Mrs Chanda (Government official's wife):**
  - Poor citizens should be provided with financial help by the state, but financial support should only cover the basic needs.
  - Citizens should be forced to take a job offer in order to sustain their right to support from the state.
  - Lazy citizens who refuse to work should not be supported anymore.
  - The government should regularly check, if regulations are obeyed.

KV 4   Orphans in India

1 The little boy is alone, playing in the dirt with rubbish, looks lonely and unhappy. Where are his parents?
Maybe people living in the streets look after him or he might be picked up by officials who will take him to an orphanage. As he is all by himself, he could easily be stolen, abused, mistreated or forgotten.

2 a Ram describes the juvenile home as an awful place. It is overcrowded, very dirty and incredibly loud. The hygienic conditions are miserable; there are only two toilets for the 150 youngsters. The children are treated badly by the custodians; there are even rumours of children being sexually abused by one of the custodians. As it turns out, nobody interferes even as the rumours are proved true.

b Some of the children have had a very hard life. They tell Ram about drug-addicted fathers and mothers who are working as prostitutes. Their faces show scars from being beaten. In addition, they have experienced abuse. For them, the juvenile home is a safe place that offers far better living conditions than they used to have at home.

c In the juvenile home, all the children talk about Sethji. He regularly comes, chooses children and takes them with him. Rumours of a fantastic life are spread in the orphanage. When Ram and Salim arrive, they are shocked. At dinner, they see all the blind children, some with missing extremities. Later, they find out that Sethji has the children crippled in order to make them more effective beggars.

d *Sample poster:*

> **Orphans in Q & A**
>
> 1. The first orphanage:
>   - miserable living conditions
>   - crowded place
>   - unhygienic conditions
>   - not enough food
>   - abuse by the custodians
>   → <u>But:</u> better than the life some of the children had before
> 2. The home for the crippled:
>   - not the happy place Ram and Salim expected
>   - children are crippled in order to make them effective beggars

The Orphan Crisis Exposed

3 The article points out many reasons why orphanned children live in danger. Nobody cares about them, so they can be abused. Unfortunately, there really are some "evil adults" who catch orphan children and cripple them in order to exploit them as beggars, who arouse people's sympathy. As living conditions in India are tough, many children are abandoned.

4 Important aspects which should be found on the internet:
- child abuse, sexual harassment and severe beatings as part of everyday life in some juvenile homes
- all right from the outside, unbearable conditions inside
- no intervention from outside to do prevent the deplorable state of affairs
- very bad living conditions, spreading of lots of illnesses
- very poor chances for orphans in life
- life in total dependence

5 Swarup presents the problems Indian orphans have to face in a realistic way.

6 Dear Sir or Madam,

I am finally well-known enough to be taken seriously. It took quite a while and loads of money to achieve this position, but never mind. I would like to use my popularity as the one and only winner of the quiz show *W3B*, to make you aware of one of the most disgusting crimes that is being committed every day on your doorstep. So please stop looking away and stay with me as I tell you about the most horrifying place I've ever been to in my entire life:

Never before have I seen such cruelty as practiced in Sethji's so-called "home for the crippled". I came to this place hoping for a better life but even the bad experiences I had already had before were topped. Sethji and his men buy children from orphanages and take them to their place. Having trained them in singing, they blind or cripple them in order to make them pitiful and financially effective beggars. The children's lives are destroyed forever. I was very lucky because I was able to escape before being crippled, but many others weren't blessed with such a lucky destiny. They suffer from physical pain due to their disfigurement and have to beg for long hours every day. To boot, they are dependent on people who have absolutely no scruples whatsoever.

Please open your eyes, have mercy and help these children! Don't pretend the misery you don't see doesn't exist! Organize help and free these children!

Yours faithfully,

Ram Mohammad Thomas

KV 5   The Wonderful World of Bollywood

1 Individual solutions

2 The man is shown twice on the poster (mirrored on a central axis), which makes him seem very dominant. Furthermore, he is pictured in the foreground and looks quite determined. The woman in the background seems to be confused or scared. She looks as if she is about to run away from someone or something. The movie is probably about a love story between the man and the woman on the poster, in which problems have to be overcome. The German title suggests that there is a ghost involved in the story.

Watching a Bollywood film scene

3 The scene is very entertaining due to the characters' dancing and singing. Beautiful women are presented, who wear a lot of jewelry and expensive saris. The scene seems to present a dream world.

Placemat activity: The real and the fictitious world of Bollywood

4 A Bollywood movies function as entertainment. By watching them, Salim escapes from his hard life. They are a contrast to his problems and worries. Armaan is a role model for Salim. Meeting Armaan in person makes Salim's illusory world become real. The encounter means a brief insight into his dream world.
Ram does not like the movie because it is too realistic. He probably likes watching unrealistic movies as he wants to see an illusory world. His aim is to get a glimpse of his personal dream world. For Ram, movies should present an illusion and therefore contrast with real life. For him they have the function of entertainment, and they provide an opportunity to escape reality for a while.

B Neelima lives in abundance. Her living conditions contrast with Ram's everyday life as she possesses everything somebody could wish for, whereas Ram lives below the poverty line.
Neelima is afraid of seeing her real face and of facing herself as a person, in contrast to playing a part in a movie. She is afraid of ageing and physically fading away.

C Ram feels privileged as the new job at Neelima's offers an insight into a star's life. But Neelima's job has taken over her real life. She embodies the illusory world that Bollywood tries to be and identifies herself with the characters she plays. Her greatest (and final) role is her suicide, which she celebrates. Her aim is to "live" and be remembered as the tragedy queen forever. For her, suicide is the only way to deal with the problem of getting older and losing her beauty.

D According to the author, Bollywood's most important function is to entertain by presenting people's emotional and social dreams. The so-called "popcorn generation" should be interested in meaning instead of low-quality entertainment. But people love to close their eyes and ignore reality instead of caring about possible solutions to the major problems.

E Possible solutions:
- entertainment
- a happy, easy world (money, love) without problems; contrast to real life
- heroes and heroines
- escape from reality
- jobs (good money, best living conditions)
- fame and fortune

After the placemat activity

5 Swarup lets Neelima die to demonstrate that the illusory world of Bollywood movies is not compatible with real life in India. Thus, whoever clings to the fictitious world of Bollywood too intensely, will fail in life.

6 Never had I thought I would become so unhappy in my life. Bollywood used to be my home, my roles used to be my life. Who am I without that illusory world which was my real life?
How can the audience just ignore me now? Don't they remember what part I used to play in their lives? They looked up to me, adored me and saw me as their idol. That's all over now. There is nothing left of all the admiration because I am not a beautiful glamorous actress any more.
A long time ago, I still remember, I had many friends and I was a happy girl running around and laughing with all the other children. But I didn't care for my old friends, didn't even call them once over the last decades. At that time I did not want to be reminded of where I came from. Only the present mattered to me. Now I only live in the past. I can't complain about being lonely now. A long time ago, I should have made the decision not to let the world of glamour totally absorb me. I should have kept my soul, but I have not. I gave it to the illusory world, as a present. But it is gone forever.
Maybe there is another chance in the afterlife. This time I will take it. I have learned my lesson. I will care for people and stick to real life rather than escape into a dream world. However, in this life there is no other solution but to go onstage for one last time and say good-bye.
Neelima Kumari

KV 6.1 **Women in India – No Chance from the very Start of their Lives?**

1 Possible answers:
- marry the man I love
- to be too rich to have to work
- have a well-paid/an interesting job
- travel a lot
- have a family, just be happy

2 Maybe, an Indian girl has the same dreams, but as the situation is very different, her dreams are not likely to come true. Poverty and being less appreciated than a boy restrict a girl's chances in life and reduce her opportunities.

3 Nita is a tribal girl from Madhya Pradesh. It is a tradition that one girl in every family works as a prostitute. As she was more beautiful than her sister, her mother chose her to fulfil that duty. Her sister meanwhile is happily married. Whereas Nita has to earn money for the family, the male members only hang around drinking and playing cards. In her current situation, Nita is helpless. If she didn't work as a prostitute, her family wouldn't have enough money to survive. She is aware of her duty to feed the family and even accepts the risk of getting infected with HIV. As she does not have a choice, she puts her happiness and health at the bottom of the list.

Being a Girl in India – A Vicious Circle

4 The vicious circle could include the following key words; the order may vary:
- bad/no education
- bad/no jobs
- poverty
- marriage at an early age
- young mothers
- less money
- bad education for the next generation

5 Text 2 makes it clear that Nita's sad story might happen in India every day. Women in general have fewer chances than men. Be it in education, at the workplace, in the families. They are considered unequal and often cannot live independently, which is why they cannot make decisions on their lives. Of course, there is always the danger of generalization. Like Gudiya, there are also a lot of well educated and independent young women in India, who have made it against all odds.

6 Possible solutions:
- The vicious circle is hard to break out of.
- Maybe there are organizations that can help.
- It's difficult to help as the inequality of women is based on traditional beliefs in Indian society.
- Small things (e.g. medical help) can help improve the living conditions.

KV 6.2 Aid Organisations for Women in India

1 Possible organizations and basic facts:

❶ **Action for World Solidarity**
- Web address: www.aswnet.de
- Basic information about the organization:
  - founded in 1957
  - financial support for self-initiated groups in India, Africa and Brazil
  - aims: improving women's living conditions and health, fighting against human trafficking and violence (especially concerning girls), protecting human rights, fighting for education and jobs for women

- Activities/Projects:
  - encouraging women to work in the field of agriculture in order to become financially independent
  - supporting help centres for abused women
  - strengthening womens' rights, organization of local support groups against trafficking in adolescent girls
- Achievements so far:
  - improved women's literacy in India
  - due to local support groups: 70 cases of human trafficking made public
  - founded the CWS (Centre of World Solidarity: supporting local NGOs, networking for the Dalits, advising peasants on agricultural issues)

❷ **Centre for Women's Development and Research**
- Web address: www.cwdr.org.in
- Basic information about the organization:
  - initiated in 1993
  - aim: increasing number of women in leading positions of NGOs
- Activities/Projects:
  - educating and organizing women
  - supporting single women and adolescent girls
  - establishing of a trade union for domestic workers
  - campaigning for women's rights
  - initiating income generation projects (e. g. catering, domestic worker job placement, soap making)
  - helping women and children after the tsunami of 2004
- Achievements so far:
  - founded a domestic workers' organization for women
  - present in 100 slums in Chennai
  - founded local networks in which women support women (focus on violence against women)
  - government lobbying to improve welfare of single women

❸ **Self Employed Women's Organization**
- Web address: www.sewa.org, www.sewadelhi.org
- Basic information about the organization:
  - registered in 1972
  - organization of poor, self-employed female workers to protect and realize their rights (e. g. savings, health and child care, insurance issues, legal aid and communications)
  - aim: help workers to become fully employed and self-reliant
- Activities/Projects:
  - vendors' campaign
  - home-based workers' campaign
  - organization and education of midwives
- Achievements so far:
  - got construction workers recognized as workers entitled to social benefits
  - secured a harassment-free market place for women in Delhi
  - established the Sewa bank with 93,000 depositors

❹ South Asian Women's Network
- Web address: www.sawnet.org
- Basic information about the organization:
  - forum where women from all over South Asia discuss women's rights
  - dedicated to politics and social and personal issues
- Activities/Projects:
  - running a mailing list (information)
  - providing a forum for discussion
  - giving women a voice
- Achievements so far:
  - informing women about their rights
  - connecting women
  - helping and encouraging women to stand up for their rights

❺ Grace Foundation
- Web address: www.gracefoundationngo.org
- Basic information about the organization:
  - Registered in 2002
  - Voluntary religious charitable organization
  - Aim: empowerment of women, child education and child labour elimination
- Activities/Projects:
  - providing medical care for the elderly
  - providing educational support
  - getting drop-outs back in school
  - giving advice on natural resources management
  - providing vocational training and community health programmes for women
  - promoting Dalit rights
- Achievements so far:
  - established 150 self-help groups
  - raised AIDS awareness
  - improvement of availability of medical treatment

2 Overall aims:
- informing society about problems women have to deal with
- providing information for women (e.g. about hygiene, contraception, HIV, diseases, rights and legal situation)
- providing sustainable and self-sustaining help, thus enabling people to help themselves (e.g. improving literacy among women, providing a network for women to communicate with each other)

Creative Writing

3 **a** *Sample e-mail:*

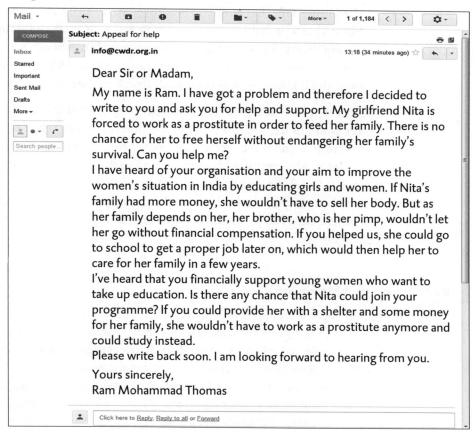

Mail ▾   ↩   ▢   ❗   🗑   ◨▾   🏷▾   More▾   1 of 1,184   ‹ ›   ⚙▾

COMPOSE

Subject: Appeal for help

Inbox
Starred
Important
Sent Mail
Drafts
More ▾

info@cwdr.org.in   13:18 (34 minutes ago) ☆   ↩ ▾

Dear Sir or Madam,

My name is Ram. I have got a problem and therefore I decided to write to you and ask you for help and support. My girlfriend Nita is forced to work as a prostitute in order to feed her family. There is no chance for her to free herself without endangering her family's survival. Can you help me?

I have heard of your organisation and your aim to improve the women's situation in India by educating girls and women. If Nita's family had more money, she wouldn't have to sell her body. But as her family depends on her, her brother, who is her pimp, wouldn't let her go without financial compensation. If you helped us, she could go to school to get a proper job later on, which would then help her to care for her family in a few years.

I've heard that you financially support young women who want to take up education. Is there any chance that Nita could join your programme? If you could provide her with a shelter and some money for her family, she wouldn't have to work as a prostitute anymore and could study instead.

Please write back soon. I am looking forward to hearing from you.

Yours sincerely,
Ram Mohammad Thomas

Click here to Reply, Reply to all or Forward

b *Sample dialogue:*

NITA: Hi! Nice to see you again! How are you? And how is your family? Oh, I see you are expecting another baby, congratulations!

FRIEND: Nice to see you, too! It's been such a long time since we last met. And you look happy, finally, after all you have been through!

NITA: It wasn't an easy time. I've always considered it my duty to follow our family's tradition and work in the brothel. I was glad I could help them to survive, at least financially. I wouldn't have dared to think of my own happiness until Ram came along. I can't believe I was so stuck in traditions and a false belief in faith that I would have sacrificed myself without batting an eye!

FRIEND: Well, I don't think all traditions are wrong. Look at me, for instance. I have married the groom of my parents' choice and I'm expecting my third child. I have done everything according to our tradition and I'm happy. It really depends on whether the tradition is based on respect or not. The person's well-being should always be the core of a custom or tradition.

NITA: You are right. And not everybody is the same. I personally can't wait to take up education and start a new life in which I am the architect of my own fortune. But I admit that you seem to be really happy, too.

FRIEND: I wouldn't want to go to school again. I am happy as a housewife and mother – but maybe only because I could have done something else as well. It's important that women are allowed to make decisions on their own lives.

NITA: That's probably the wisest thing you have ever said! *(laughs in a friendly way)* Sorry, I have to leave. I have an appointment at a school; they want to get to know me before they offer me a position. Wish me luck!

FRIEND: I'll keep my fingers crossed! Bye, Nita. See you again soon.

4 The fact that Nita doesn't even have a surname symbolizes the lack of identity she suffers from. In her job as a prostitute it doesn't matter who she is and where she comes from as she is reduced to her body. She accepts her destiny but sounds bitter about it. She compares herself to pets that don't have a surname either. Like them, she fulfills her function but isn't free.

When she marries Ram in the end, she proudly takes on his surname. In doing so she starts a new life in which she will matter as a person. Now she is a complete human being.

KV 7   Arranged Marriages

1 Indian society seems to be very religious and traditional as the first matrimonial points out the groom's caste membership. Nevertheless, it also claims that the family has liberal religious views. Family background seems to be important, and the first ad focuses on the groom's outward appearance.

In contrast to this, the second matrimonial seems to place more value on the professional (and thus economic/financial) situation of the groom and the future bride. However, this family must also be very traditional as they are looking for a (probably Indian) bride in an Indian newspaper although the groom seems to be living in Britain.

2 Individual solutions

Expertenpuzzle

3 Group A:

Love is not the most important priority, and arranged marriages are seen as a necessity due to social and economic factors. The aim is to have a stable marriage. It is believed that love can grow with time.

Parents choose their children's partners as they know their offspring best. Therefore, they are likely to make the perfect choice. Low divorce rates among arranged marriages prove this theory. Nevertheless, the small number of divorces shouldn't be taken too seriously as an argument for arranged marriages as people in India usually do not get divorced anyway.

Group B:

Lakshmi's future husband should be good-looking. In addition, he should have a respectable family and a good job. These aspects should guarantee Lakshmi a good life with him.

Lajwanti has to provide the dowry for Lakshmi. She has saved a lot of money and is planning on borrowing the rest. As Rani Sahiba, who she works for, refuses to give her the money, she decides to steal a necklace from her employer in order to be able to satisfy the groom's family's demands.

4 Swarup focuses on the problems connected with arranged marriages but doesn't question the concept. Due to this hidden criticism he seems to convey a fairly modern attitude towards arranged marriages.

Talk show

5 Possible arguments **against** arranged marriages:
- Parents might decide on their children's partners only because of the other family's reputation. Thus, young people may be forced into a marriage they really do not want. (Samir Bhatnagar, Rajani Charan)
- Marriage should be based on true love. (Samir, Rajani, Steve King)
- Negative aspects regarding the bride or groom could be hidden by the respective family. (Steve)
- In general, parents should not decide on their children's partner as they do not have to live with the spouse for the rest of their lives. (Samir, Rajani)

Possible arguments **in favour of** arranged marriages:
- As parents decide on the marriage, there will be full family support in case of any personal or financial crisis. Moreover, the two families might become very close and support the young couple together. (Mr Bhatnagar)
- There is no need to chase after boys or girls as the partner will be chosen by the family anyway. In addition, even girls and boys who are not exceptionally beautiful will get a suitable partner. (Mrs Bhatnagar)
- As most arranged marriages do not cross the boundaries between the social and economic classes, classes do not mix. (Mr Bhatnagar)
- Marriages are arranged between people of the same culture, religious belief and maybe personal background. That can help to reduce possible future problems within the couple's relationship. (Mrs Bhatnagar)

6 Individual solutions

7
— The Tribune Matrimonials —
Lakshmi, beautiful girl. Handsome boy preferred.
Respectable family background and secure financial situation required.
Contact Lajwanti, c/o Rani Sahiba, Agra.

KV 8 Tourism and Travelling in India

Ram's Journey through India

1 Travelling in India seems to be very different from travelling in Germany; there is no such thing as comfort; it's more like fighting for a tiny space to squeeze in. The train is packed with people, even on the roof; there are many passengers. Safety does not seem to be a topic of relevance as Ram and Salim are shown hanging around between the wagons and on the roof.
The train seems to be very slow, so travelling in India must take ages. People seem to live on the train. They sleep, eat, have fun, sell and buy goods.

2 a • Ram encounters tourists in Agra when he works as a guide at the Taj Mahal. This is one of the most famous tourist attractions in India. Visiting the Taj Mahal is the tourists' only intention when coming to Agra.
  • Western Tourists are presented as arrogant, superficial and boastful with their money. They are usually equipped with technical gadgets and want to have fun on holiday (e.g. enjoy the cheap prices, drinks and women). They also seem ignorant of Indian history and culture as well as of their own.
  • Ram feels shy, overwhelmed by their financial capabilities, happy to earn money, fascinated by a lifestyle that would be unaffordable for him.

b Ram's journeys:
  • From Delhi to Mumbai: Chosen by Warden Sahib and taken to "home for the crippled".
  • From Mumbai to Delhi to escape from the police because he hit Mr Shantaram in Ghatkopar who fell off the first floor.
  • From Delhi to Agra (planned destination: Mumbai) to see Salim; Ram gets off earlier because of certain events on the train.
  • From Agra to Mumbai to forget the sad memories Ram associates with Agra.

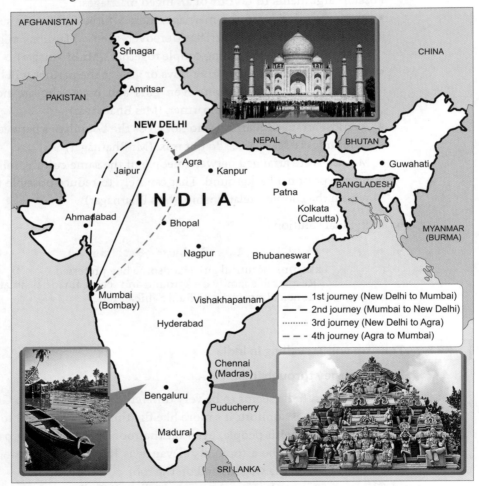

Tourism and Travelling in India – Background information

3 In general, both foreign and domestic tourism have increased in India between 2008 and 2010. Domestic tourism in India has increased steadily in the last ten years. Between 2008 and 2010, figures have grown from about 550 million to over 700 million Indian people visiting the different Indian States every year (cf. table 4). Western Europeans are by far the largest tourist group with figures constantly over 1.6 million visitors from 2008 to 2010 (cf. table 1). It is remarkable that the second largest number of tourists (those from North America) has grown considerably from about one million visitors in 2008 to almost 1.2 million in 2010. The figures of other tourist groups increase steadily as well, while the numbers of Asian and European visitors decreased slightly in 2009, only to reach a new high in 2010.

4 India is most popular with tourists aged 35 to 44 years as table 2 suggests. They represent over 20 per cent of all tourists in 2010. The second largest group are foreign visitors aged 45 to 54, followed by tourists in their late twenties and early thirties. It seems very likely that those groups can, on the one hand, afford the expensive flight to India, while they are also flexible enough to cope with the chaotic public transport, the foreign food and culture. They are more likely to adapt to circumstances than the age groups over 55.

5 The majority of Indians spend their holiday in India. Compared to over 700 million Indians who travel within the country, only a small number travels to foreign countries (cf. tables 3 and 4). The reason for this phenomenon might be simple: Lots of Indians are quite poor and cannot afford expensive holidays. Moreover, those travelling to national destinations might either visit relatives, famous places nearby, or travel to religious spots as pilgrims. Almost all of the most popular destinations for international flights are located in the Middle, or Far East, e. g. Kuwait, Singapore, Malaysia and China amongst the top five. The only exceptions are flights to the US, the fourth most popular destination of Indian people. Again, flights to those Asian countries might not be so expensive and Indians might find it easier to adapt to the culture than to the Western way of living and eating.

6 Swarup pictures the tourists rather critically as they do not seem to be interested in the "real" India but only in the romanticized places and cheap holidays. Therefore, he might want to point out our appalling behaviour abroad, which is insensitive because we close our eyes instead of trying to improve the situation of the poor in India.

7 Advantages	Disadvantages
• totally different lifestyle: getting to know a different culture and a different way of life • enriching experience to broaden one's horizon • developing a different attitude on one's own life • getting to know new people • discovering the "real" India • lots of places to visit	• unable to speak Hindi or another Indian language • dangerous and unknown surroundings • different preferences concerning travel spots • danger of catching foreign illnesses

KV 9.1 | **Q & A on Screen – *Slumdog Millionaire***

1

	Novel	Movie
Means of conveying a plot	• many options for conveying the thoughts of the characters (e.g. interior monologue, dialogue, omniscient narrator, reported speech)	• limited options for conveying the thoughts of the characters due to spoken language (e.g. dialogue, narrator's voice offstage) • pictures (including facial expressions and gestures)
Advantages	• pictures formed by imagination • plot influenced by reader's imagination	• emotional via audio-visual means (music, pictures, voices …) • development of clear ideas of a foreign world • setting and plot more palpable
Disadvantages	• only visual way to take in information • no visual images of settings	• audience guided very tightly • no (less) individual interpretation of the plot

2

Novel	Movie
• The orphanage is pictured negatively: Ram and Salim are shocked when they see all the "crippled" children. • Ram and Salim only overhear Maman's plan on crippling them both the following night and flee afterwards (there is more time in-between the single events). • The boys only see the result of the crippling.	• The arrival at the orphanage is pictured very positively: Ram (Jamal) and Salim seem to be overwhelmed by the happy place. • The crippling of a child is shown directly. Ram (Jamal) and Salim are shocked and manage to escape (the events happen soon after each other). • Salim assists when another boy called Arvind is blinded.

3 By showing shocking scenes, the film makes the boys' misery more visible, and one feels for them. The pictures and the use of music move the audience. The movie seems to follow the principle of "black or white": the distinction between the helpless boys and the men who want to exploit them becomes huge. Thus, the contradiction between good and evil is made even more obvious. Also, scenes are cut faster and one action follows soon after the other.

Evaluating film and novel

4 Western people were positively overwhelmed as Ram's (Jamal's) victory over corruption, poverty and discrimination won their hearts. They were shocked and touched by the misery depicted in the movie. In India hostile attitudes towards the movie were based mainly on the title *Slumdog Millionaire* as it was considered to be discriminating. One man even filed a law suit against the title of the film.

5 The movie seems to focus on Ram's (Jamal's) fight against "evil India". Poor people are not only pictured as victims of the system, but also very often in a negative light, such as the boss of the orphanage. Some people might be afraid that their country will get a bad image because of the film.
Furthermore, the main aim of making this film was very likely to achieve as much turnover as possible. A heart-breaking story like Ram's (Jamal's) is therefore rather a means to reach this aim. To fight poverty hardly was the producer's main goal.

6 *Slumdog Millionaire* pictures India through Western eyes and is shot in a very eye-catching way. Therefore, it might a bit one-sided and not too realistic concerning Jamal's fate. But it authentically depicts India from one possible perspective, which is absolutely legitimate. Thanks to the film, Western people might become aware of the some of the real problems in India which can be a first step towards solving them.

Of course, the title of the film is a bit sensational and can cause offence. On the other hand, many people might have become aware of the film due to its catchy title in the first place. "Slumdog" might not be the name slum-dwellers would pick for themselves, but if the film casts a realistic light on social interactions in India, this is what the residents of places like Dharavi are called by the middle and the upper class. If this is true, it is Indian society that is degrading the slum-dwellers and not the director Danny Boyle, who merely borrowed the word from colloquial Indian slang. Still, "slumdog" is a pejorative word and should cease to be used.

7 Arguments **in favour of** reading *Q & A* as a means of discovering India:
- realistic portrayal of India: from rich to poor, fortunate to unfortunate, the novel covers a wide range of topics and the reader gets to know interesting characters from various backgrounds
- motivation to find out more about India: as the plot moves on quickly, each episode is touched on quite superficially thus leaving the reader to find out more about this fascinating country

Arguments **against** reading *Q & A* as a means of discovering India:
- stories as superficial episodes: the quick pace in which the stories follow one another prevents the reader from getting a real insight into the workings of Indian society. The novel can merely serve as a trigger to explore the topic of India in more depth later on.
- Swarup as a shallow author: the novel only portrays Indian society, leaving words of criticism entirely to the reader. It is rather suggested that these examples of injustice will be levelled by fate in the end: likeable Ram marries the woman of his dreams in the end, Smita clears Ram of all charges against him, Lajwanti gets out of jail and evil quiz master Kumar dies.

KV 9.2 **India – A Jigsaw Puzzle**

chaotic
way of
travelling

history of the
Taj Mahal

tragic lot of
the orphans

inequality between
men and women

excessive corruption

religious
conflicts

Concept
of arranged
marriages

fairy-tale world
of Bollywood

extreme poverty vs.
extreme wealth

Indian way
to make
do

KV 10 **Klausurvorschlag mit Erwartungshorizont**

Comprehension/Analysis

1 Most Indians, including many poor people, celebrated the international success of the film *Slumdog Millionaire*. According to them, the movie has raised international awareness regarding poverty and living conditions in India. The movie does not sugarcoat Indian reality but shows harsh reality and many of the problems poor people in India have to deal with every day. The actors were celebrated as heroes as they were considered the ones to have brought India into the international community's focus.

However, the movie did not evoke positive responses alone. Opponents object to the movie, claiming that India is presented far too negatively. They consider the title *Slumdog Millionaire* discriminating. Furthermore, they claim the movie only shows problems and the absence of human rights instead of offering a well-balanced image of India.

In addition to that, critical voices predict that the international interest will not be of great duration but will vanish in time. Thus, the poor in India will enjoy international recognition and help only briefly.

2 Bollywood movies tend to present an illusory world in which luck and love are omnipresent. Lovers manage to overcome sometimes even life-threatening problems with ease, awful living conditions are banned from the screen, and only happiness and wealth weave through the plot. This presentation of an unrealistic glamorous world functions as an escape from reality for many Indian people. This can be seen in the novel Q & A in which Ram and especially his friend Salim love watching Bollywood movies as this makes it possible for them to forget about their hard lives for a while. The movies take them on a journey into a world of joy, mentally leading them far away from reality.

In contrast to those movies, *Slumdog Millionaire* shows reality with a focus on authentic problems. By doing so, it contradicts the idea of Bollywood. The main characters manage only slowly, and not always, to overcome the obstacles that prevent them from succeeding to be happy. Only at the last minute do they manage to reach their goal and save their lives.

Bollywood movies, as well as *Slumdog Millionaire*, focus on only one side and could therefore be accused of picturing India in a biased way. They reduce India to an either (mostly) positive or negative image.

Comment

3 Possible argumentation:

- Introduction:

  Some politicians are thinking about demolishing the biggest slum in Mumbai, Dharavi. They want to introduce a redevelopment plan, which has caused great opposition among the inhabitants of Dharavi. They want their slum, which is their home, to be preserved instead of being knocked down. Many of them are glad to have found a home in Dharavi which saves them from living in the streets without any protection. They do not believe in the government redevelopment plan and are afraid of being completely homeless once Dharavi has become history.

- Main part (alternatives):
  - In my opinion, Dharavi offers the inhabitants at least a bearable place to live and should be preserved ...
  - In my opinion, living in Dharavi must be like living in hell, and it should be demolished ...

  Possible arguments **in favour of** Dharavi as a place to live:
  - provides a social network (solidarity)
  - offers jobs
  - offers at least very basic accommodation

  Possible arguments **against** Dharavi as a place to live:
  - almost unbearable living conditions
  - poor sanitation = spread of diseases
  - no privacy

- Conclusion (alternatives):
  - As I have shown above, Dharavi can function as a home for the inhabitants and should be preserved by the government. Instead of coming up with a redevelopment plan, the state should try to improve the living conditions in the existing slum and take the inhabitants' wishes to stay seriously.
  - As I have pointed out above, Dharavi cannot be seen as a bearable home for the inhabitants and should be demolished. The government should quickly refine the redevelopment plan and try to realize it as soon as possible. By relocating the inhabitants, many lives could be saved. Knocking down Dharavi and moving the people to a different place is the only possible course of action that will help the people of Dharavi and respects their human rights.

Bildnachweis

Umschlag: © imago/Unimedia Images

S. 25: © vectomart/123rf

S. 27 (oben links nach unten rechts): Wikimedia, Photographer: erin; this file is licensed under the Creative Commons Attribution 2.0 Generic.; Wikimedia, Photographer: Kounosu; this file is licensed under the GNU Free Documentation License, Version 1.2 or any later version; © Indranil Mukherjee/AFP/Getty Images; Wikimedia, Photographer: Abhinav Saxena; this file is licensed under the Creative Commons Attribution 2.0 Generic.; © Digitalfestival/Dreamstime.com; © Digitalfestival/Dreamstime.com

S. 28: **Slum:** Wikimedia, Photographer: Jason Turner; this file is licensed under the Creative Commons Attribution 2.0 Generic.; **Ganesha:** © Katya Ulitina/123rf

S. 29, 39, 44/45: © Katya Ulitina/123rf

S. 31, 32: © Arvind Balaraman/123rf

S. 33, 52, 74: © Judith Christina Säckl

S. 35: © Nadezda Korobkova/123rf

S. 36: © www.redchillies.com

S. 37: © Arminaudovenko/Dreamstime.com

S. 38: © tang90246/123rf

S. 40: © Dennis Richardson/Dreamstime.com

S. 41: © Samrat35/Dreamstime.com

S. 43, 45/46, 69: © Cezary Gwozdz/Dreamstime

S. 46: © Omer Nusrullah/123rf

S. 47, 70: **Kerala Küste:** David Rodriguez/123rf; **Taj Mahal:** © Sushi King/Fotolia.com; **Chennai Temple:** © jorisvo/123rf; **Karte:** © Redaktion

S. 49: © Oleksiy Mark/123rf

S. 50: **Bücherstapel:** © MC/Fotolia.com; **Filmklappe:** © Emin Ozkan/Dreamstime